COVID GARDENS

COVID GARDENS

THE ANTI-POEMS OF STARK HUNTER

BY STARK HUNTER

Copyright 2021 by Stark Hunter

Paperback ISBN: 978-1-63337-545-1
E-Book ISBN: 978-1-63337-532-1
LCCN: 2021918819

Published by Mind Tavern Books

All rights reserved. No part of this book may be reproduced or transmitted in any form or by any means, electronic or mechanical, including photocopying, recording, or by any information storage and retrieval system, without permission in writing from the copyright owners.

Photographs from the Stark Hunter Collection.

ACKNOWLEDGEMENTS AND DETRITUS

SO, WHAT IS "ANTI-POETRY?" According to the scribes of Wikipedia, it is "an art movement that attempts to break away from the normal conventions of traditional poetry." Further, "anti-poems have been described as prose-like, irreverent, and illuminating the problems of human existence." These anti-literature "may have intentionally-made mistakes in regard to prosody, grammar and rhyme."

Apparently there are Anti-Poet "fathers and gurus" from the 20th Century I need to acknowledge and thank, but no AntiPoet worth his salt would do such a patronizing, crass thing, so I won't.

However, I do acknowledge a ghost as my chief source of inspiration. Her photo stares at me in my 'cave of writing"— She tells me to screw everyone else, and to write the damn thing for myself. I did…

Dedicated to Gertrude Stein

STARK HUNTER, 11/20

POET'S INSTRUCTIONS:

THANK YOU FOR READING this 12th volume of my writings. You are kindly asked to follow all the instructions contained therein as you read this work. By doing this, you will be following CDC guidelines and protocols; plus, your poetic experience within will be enriched and intensified.

Photo by Hunter

ANTI-INTRODUCTIONS

ENGLISH

Really? You want an introduction to these skin warts? These cankerous bleedings from someplace I cannot see? Well, suffice it to say, these lesions were penned on a tablet in 2020 during the COVID-19 world pandemic. I consider this volume to be "Covid Literature," written in quarantine; Herewith submitted,
Stark Hunter
November, 2020

FRENCH

Vraiment? Vous voulez une introduction à ces verrues cutanées? Ces saignements chanceux d'un endroit que je ne vois pas? Eh bien, il suffit de dire que ces lésions ont été écrites sur une tablette en 2020 lors de la pandémie mondiale COVID-19. Je considère ce volume comme de la littérature Covid, écrite en quarantaine; Soumis par la présente,
Stark Hunter
Novembre 2020

SPANISH

De Verdad? ¿Quieres una introducción a estas verrugas cutáneas? ¿Estos sangrados canceros de algún lugar que no puedo ver? Bueno, basta con decir que estas lesiones se escribieron en una tableta en 2020 durante la pandemia mundial COVID-19. Considero que este volumen es Covid Literature, escrito en cuarentena; Adjunto enviado,
Stark Hunter
Noviembre de 2020

TABLE OF CONTENTS

Anti-Poem 1:	"Of Monkey Face and Hooker's Lips"	1
Anti-Poem 2:	"Mister Aranda"	3
Anti-Poem 3:	"Allen Funt, I'm Surprised You Aren't Dead Yet"	4
Anti-Poem 4:	"The Glinting Candles"	6
Anti-Poem 5:	"Dying Is Not On The Agenda"	8
Anti-Poem 6:	"Eddie And The Showmen"	10
Anti-Poem 7:	"Santo and Johnny"	14
Anti-Poem 8:	"Veronica Lake's Meat Loaf"	17
Anti-Poem 9:	"The Dying Nurse"	20
Anti-Poem 10:	"Johnny Ace In Heaven"	22
Anti-Poem 11:	"Savoy Brown at the Swing"	24
Anti-Poem 12:	"The Dream Palace"	26
Anti-Poem 13:	"Experiment For Two Mouths And One Ear"	28
Anti-Poem 14:	"Headless Jesus"	29
Anti-Poem 15:	"Dancing Cheek To Cheek"	31
Anti-Poem 16:	"Quarantined"	34
Anti-Poem 17:	"Living In A Netflix Movie"	36
Anti-Poem 18:	"Hieronymus Bosch Wakes Up"	38
Anti-Poem 19:	"Something Lurking In Clapham Common"	41
Anti-Poem 20:	"Sniffing A Coroner's Van"	43
Anti-Poem 21:	"The Bambino"	46
Anti-Poem 22:	"Johnny Ray Tiptoes"	48
Anti-Poem 23:	"The It"	50
Anti-Poem 24:	"Riding Suburban Shotgun"	53
Anti-Poem 25:	"Watering The Grass"	55
Anti-Poem 26:	"Empty Chair"	58
Anti-Poem 27:	"Mosquito Music"	60
Anti-Poem 28:	"Apache"	63

Anti-Poem 29: "Apocalyptic Sinatra" 65
Anti-Poem 30: "The Murmaids" 68
Anti-Poem 31: "Illinois" 72
Anti-Poem 32: "Pulsing Humans" 74
Anti-Poem 33: "Harry the Hipster" 75
Anti-Poem 34: "Linda Keene - The Unlucky Woman" 77
Anti-Poem 35: "End of the World" 80
Anti-Poem 36: "You Want That Burger?" 84
Anti-Poem 37: "The Skies Outside Ooze" 86
Anti-Poem 38: "Woodstock Boogie" 88
Anti-Poem 39: "Mistinguett" 90
Anti-Poem 40: "Rita Montero" 92
Anti-Poem 41: "Our Winter Love" 94
Anti-Poem 42: "Free Form Guitar" 96
Anti-Poem 43: "Autumn Postcards" 99
Anti-Poem 44: "Mona Lisa" 103
Anti-Poem 45: "Silent Mercies" 105
Anti-Poem 46: "Screaming Requiems?" 108
Anti-Poem 47: "Sugar Plums" 110
Anti-Poem 48: "Mother Dearest" 112
Anti-Poem 49: "So Rare" 114
Anti-Poem 50: "Last Night" 116
Anti-Poem 51: "Miasma Clouds" 118
Anti-Poem 52: "The Poem That Does Not Exist" 119
The Last Page: 120
About the Author 121

ANTI-POEM 1
"OF MONKEY FACE AND HOOKER'S LIPS"

(Poet's Instruction: Please play "Morceaux" by
Tchaikovsky, while reading this anti-poem)

Can you hear the distant piano music?
Listen.

It is the Morceaux by Tchaikovsky.
Let us meander down this path,
Leading to the outcropping of flat blades.
Let us make our comfortable way,
Under these fawning birch trees,
These crowned inviolable flowers,
Of monkey face and hooker's lips
Striving beneath and behind ancient stones
Dotting the way.
Let us pass this old graveyard
Which gate is locked,
We mustn't allow its listless shadows
To touch us, subdue us.
We mustn't stoop and stare inside
These naked earthen confines.
Here now is a blue stream in the sun,
Vibrant with rushing certitudes,
Rich in wisdom-fish,
Thriving under safe currents.
Now we come to the great plain,

COVID GARDENS

A grassy plain, as vast as the sea squared;
A single door in the distance stands ajar.
All of humanity is mulling here,
Chatting and eating incessantly,
Swallowing empty phraseologies,
Swilling carnivorous rhetoric;
Waiting for their number to be called.
Waiting to take the long stiff walk,
The dreaded one all humans will take,
Traversing this green velvet plain,
Heading to the death door, over there.
Hear the music now?

It is Tchaikovsky humming in distorted whispers;
Conducting his crescendoing human meltdown,
Under the black belly of those stars,
Under these fawning birch trees,
These crowned inviolable flowers,
Of monkey face and hooker's lips.

STARK HUNTER

ANTI-POEM 2
"MISTER ARANDA"

(Poet's Instruction- You are to read this anti-poem aloud. Absolutely no silent readings of this work are allowed.)

I am riding fast through supersonic time,
Back to 1986 inside a shadowy classroom,
Gazing out a Venetian window at Mister Aranda.
He is trimming the Annabelles by the practice field.
I can hear young-voiced people in a catholic crowd.
I can hear jet airplanes flying hurriedly overhead.
I can smell the spaghetti sauce wafting at noon,
Emanating from the small side dining room,
Where old teachers sit huddled at round tables,
Under the closed dead eyes of Jesus Christ crucified.
Priests wearing black trousers stroll the green grounds.
Nuns in stern habits and dark hosiery whisper words.
They pray together in the cold, holding rosary beads,
Chanting the prayers of the dead and the long-buried,
Singing a cappello in the square of spectating junipers.
Mister Aranda with thin black mustache clips and chops,
Maneuvering old garden shears with gray pleated gloves,
The packed dry hedge of hornbeam, and bristling boxwood.

COVID GARDENS

ANTI-POEM 3
"ALLEN FUNT, I'M SURPRISED YOU AREN'T DEAD YET"

"Walmart's run outta meat,
And the National Guard is rolling inta town!
This ain't no joke Grandma Zora!
I seen them cops walking down my street last night,
Sniffing 'round like hungry dogs loose on the scent."

"Ah, is this for real?
Is there a hidden camera somewhere close by?
Is it behind that truck or in the bakery window?
Is this Candid Camera?
Am I on national tv right now?
Come out of there, Allen Funt, you can't fool me!
Come on dude, where are you hiding?
I'm surprised you aren't dead yet.
Only you could dream up this strange idea,
This unbelievable stunt to boost your sagging ratings.
Hey, you ought to pitch it to Rod Serling, man!"

"You seen them insane lines at Costco?
Damn clear 'round the building in the rain!
I ain't standing in the freaking rain to buy toilet paper!
Do I look dumb to you? Maybe I do.
But I ain't dumb when I say,
Them cops is dragging people out,
Ain't dumb to say they're being taken away in black hummers.
I ain't kidding!"

STARK HUNTER

"Hey Durward Kirby, are you in the audience tonight?
Maybe Bess Myerson is back there behind the curtain,
Maybe she's arguing on the phone with her husband.
I would feel better about all this if Bess
Would just get off the phone!
Get off the freaking phone!
And pay attention to America watching you!
Pay attention to the sea of eyes staring in,
Like renegade marbles on a blank slate,
Staring and peering in at you with laser perceptions,
Unraveling the truth from your bacon cheeseburger.
Hey Allen Funt, you rascal you!
Where are you hiding the camera these days?
Are you sure you're dead and buried?
In that unknown grave of yours?"

"If them beady-eyed varmints come on my land I'll get my gun!
Come on! Come to my front door and I will spit in your face!
How's 'bout a bullet milkshake for breakfast since yer here anyways?
Hey! You guys got a freaking search warrant? Let me see it!
I tell ya Grandma Zora, them guys mean business with their cold stares,
Their tanks and them fancy machine guns they tote around like rakes.
I seen them boys cut down a tree with just bullet rounds spraying it in half.
Like it was some kind of weird-ass magic trick from hell but it's real!
Come on! Come and get me!
Tell your uncle Jake to close the garden gate cus' of them varmints."

COVID GARDENS

ANTI-POEM 4
"THE GLINTING CANDLES"

(Poet's Instruction: Due to the creepy subject matter of the following, you are hereby forbidden to read this anti-poem. Please turn the page now).

No, I did not look.
Why would I want to watch you?
Why would I even desire you?
You are a beautiful tuna fish sandwich.
A walking duffle bulging with ephemera.
There isn't any rush though.
The clock on my wrist sweats.
Perhaps we will fly tomorrow.
Perhaps we will fly yesterday.

There is no time in a slaughter house.
No hope of seeing an emergent rise.
See there! Look over by the dogwood.
It is a blonde virgin sleeping on the grass.
Her painting of a young girl isn't finished yet.
A chipped soap dish with chlorophyll lye,
Sits by her bathtub of snowy cast iron, as
She bathes wondrously on a naked Saturday.

No, I did not look.
I did not spy through
Her open gaping window.

STARK HUNTER

Did not peer through
Glinting candles on her bare sill,
This singing virgin dance,
I did not spy upon I swear.
Did not squint my eyes
To watch her bathe alone there,
Nor did I peep with
Appalling gasps at this curious virgin,
Cleansing and rubbing unctuously,
Her sweet-smelling soaps and unguents.
To God in heaven I swear,
I did not secretly gaze there,
Upon the virgin's curvaceous signatures,
Carved upon the finest of young boxwood,
This ripe document of exquisite stories untold,
Deeply and painstakingly etched there;
The quill in her probing hand.
The ink finding new exclamations.

No, I did not look.
Why would I want to see you shudder?
Why would I even desire to do so?
Perhaps we will fly tomorrow.
Perhaps we will fly yesterday.

COVID GARDENS

ANTI-POEM 5
"DYING IS NOT ON THE AGENDA"

You know only one thing and that is:
Dying is not on the agenda.

Let us march now inside St. Mary's,
March reverently through these green repentant doors,
These holy portals to grace and absolution,
Into a stain-glassed sanctuary of sinners kneeling in disguise,
These sullied souls coming in through the out door again,
Figuring death is furloughed from the crucifixion business,
Two thousand blurry years later.
Let us still march forward now to the glassed tabernacle,
Resting up there ensconced upon the marble altar,
Beyond human touch;
The host inside now transubstantiating as with earthen time,
From dry crusty oatmeal,
To omnipotent King of the Universe.

The boy holds his new Sunday missal,
As the family drives to ancient St. Joseph's,
Up the asphalt hill, there on Gold Street,
Amidst the tentative Yuletide presentations,
Of tinsel-lit trees and blinking avenue abodes.
In the distance Lady Lassen wears a white bonnet,
As the Redding Christmas Tree stands exuberant,
Seventy-three feet into the icy air on Market Street,
A rainbow-glowing giant with a thousand staring eyes.

STARK HUNTER

Brenda Lee is singing,
Rocking Around the Christmas Tree,
From blaring radios inside Oldsmobiles and Studebakers,
Cruising Placer Street to the Cascade showing Butterfield 8.

The boy is counting the neon cocktails,
While riding in the backseat on blue polyurethane,
His father is intently driving the blue '58 impala,
Into a gravelly hilltop parking lot.
Blaring outward from the church there I heard voices,
A bubbling sacramental bouillabaisse of silent
Parishioners all genuflecting in pristine Latin confusion.
The girls choir wearing skirts of curious plaid, is
Singing loudly and softly their angelic vocal renderings:
"Gloria in excelsis Deo"
Father Elliot is extending his arms outward now,
Bestowing the final expectant blessing;
He is giving absolution to the captives driving Cadillacs.

You know only one thing and that is:
Dying is not on the agenda.

COVID GARDENS

ANTI-POEM 6
"EDDIE AND THE SHOWMEN"

Eddie and the Showmen are jamming in the back room,
Playing Mr. Rebel electrically,
Upon the boy's turning record player,
As his mother sizzles yellow eggs,
In a teflon skillet singing,
The Anniversary Waltz.
A banjo sleeps catlike in the corner.
There are eggbeaters looking to be heard,
As with loud rattles,
At dawn shaken by insistent infants,
Seeking a purpose and a redress,
As laboring men drive gas guzzlers,
To neon-lit burger stands,
Patrolled by teen girls on skates,
Flashing shadowy cleavages and chili fries,
Desperate for electric embraces,
Behind saliva doors made of man skin;
They sit together now at sidewalk cafes
Looking to laugh at nothing,
Attempting to ignite another heartbeat,
In the vicinity of nowhere.

Eddie and the Showmen are bringing it all back to me!
The smells and aromas of frying Rice A Roni,
Creeping down the hallway,
Like curious cats stalking mice,

STARK HUNTER

In a dark night of games and blood,
They strum and beat sounds,
From the back room of sausage time;
1964, before Mass at St. Mary's,
We glided into the asphalt parking lot,
And followed the white painted lines,
To the angels of Mary at her assumption.
We stayed in line for holy communion,
Wearing black shoes and white shirts,
Receiving the wafer upon extending tongues;
Now I am remembering the touch of his finger,
His sanctified appendage within a scant second,
Of spirit and spit intermingling,
Like eggs and tears.
The Rice A Roni is done,
So remove the cover and turn off the burner.
She is sitting in my place wearing nothing.
What to make of that?
But it is not about her protruding firm breasts,
Her soft perfumed fountains,
Spiraling hot spumes beyond,
The echo music and the salt-tasting.
Nor is it about her open mouth,
Seeking a cool drink from the darkness.
It is about no one living nowhere,
Doing nothing in a universe of dust.

(Stop! Poet Instruction: Play "Mr. Rebel"
through completely. Then continue reading)

COVID GARDENS

Eddie and the Showmen are striking up the band,
Playing erect guitars,
Playing mouth harps made of reed teeth
From eels of dark blond desires;

(Keep reading here, it gets juicy)

They are traipsing down the dark hallway unzipping,
Undressing unhurriedly in the mindless moment,
To find unspoken blood pleasures.
Now we are hearing The Who,
Blasting their electric orgasms from Leeds in 1970,
With spasming guitars and heaving drums,
Screaming maniacally of the unzippings,
Inside dark, wine-stinking Volkswagens,
With probing fingers pointing and prodding
Curious girls, dressed in tight cotton dresses,
Splashed of red tie dye, redolent of Heaven Scent.
"Hey, I know those girls!
I picked them up on the boulevard,
Just a half century ago."
But they are young and firm again,
Jiggling wondrously, and now, I am Prufrock.
I am walking invisibly past the naked mermaids,
Indeed, they are singing each to each.
Have they all died out finally,
Leaving me alone here to find no one at twilight time?
I miss my dead friends from 1970, but
I can see them carousing inside the graveyard,
Speaking loudly their warnings from the tombstones,

STARK HUNTER

Like trumpets of disaster looming in Leeds.
Shhh! Listen. I can hear them from my new grave,
Here, in the nothing blackness,
Eddie and the Showmen playing Mr. Rebel again,
In the vicinity of nowhere.

COVID GARDENS

ANTI-POEM 7
"SANTO AND JOHNNY"

(Poet's instruction- Play "Sleepwalk" twice
by Santo and Johnny while reading)

Santo and Johnny play Sleepwalk on Fender steel and bass
Just oozing out their mellow electric dream sound as the
Santa Monica Pier exudes under a blue napkin of sky voices
Lifting tanned bodies aloft into the maelstrom of sun and stars
The world sneezes and belches out high octane cries of desire
Armed with young ideas and brittle baskets of sunset lovemaking
Democrats and Republicans engorge the sun with rum and cigars
As Johnny and Lana drink lizard-shoe cocktails at the Formosa
The Platters glide across the cathode sky
singing Smoke Gets In Your Eyes
The '58 impala cruises at 75 miles per hour with Bobby Rydell driving

Jackie Robinson hits a liner against the Tydol sign at Ebbets
He rounds second base with cleats digging into the hard ground
Driving home Pee Wee Reese in the roaring Flatbush shadows
Democrats and Republicans devour frankfurters
and drink tequila al fresco
As Joe and his wife meet Bogie for beers and cigarettes behind third
There Jackie Robinson stands in an indomitable black sheen of sweat
Muscular as a lion bent on the kill by a river he dances the line fantastic
This magnificent eagle taloned for the high ascendances without wings
Santo and Johnny sit in the bleachers searching for beauty and truth as
Preacher Roe walks in from the bullpen with his lanky spitter spinning

STARK HUNTER

Abraham Zapruder climbs a white abutment
in Dealey Plaza wearing black
The Midnight Blue is turning on Elm and
now it is showtime in 1963
Twenty-six seconds of a national nightmare
a Bell & Howell blood orgy as
Miss Sitzman throttles his business attire
from behind steadying his hand
Democrats and Republicans wave to a legend
and take screaming Polaroids
Santo and Johnny play Sleepwalk
to the gasping pigeons who scatter like flies
The Babushka Lady insists on playing The Singing Nun
as morticians gather
Brain matter and roses spray the Dallas denizens
as they flee to the bullets
Jackie decides on second thought
to retrieve the husband's brain in the roar
Miss America stops waving
and Bert Parks stops singing the deed is done

Santo and Johnny have tamed the Cooper Hawks
they have bowed their heads
As Santo glides his steel fingers
across the American landscape of gun violence
Father Flanagan herds his boys for the big cakewalk
in a drawn circle of death
Democrats and Republicans will dutifully carry their Captain
to his deep grave
They are the broken-hearted fathers and brothers

COVID GARDENS

seeking another close dance
Another flirtation with new nights dallying
with pillbox ladies wearing pink roses
The sun is forever setting in Dealey Plaza
as the black phantom hearse drives by
Again and again for an eternity of unending gaspings
by the stunned witnesses
Sleepwalk is playing through the pergola loudspeakers
now in the autumn dusk
As undead ghosts cry alone again
astride the green expanse of lawn and life

STARK HUNTER

ANTI-POEM 8
"VERONICA LAKE'S MEAT LOAF"

(Poet's Instruction- Do not read this anti-poem unless you have received both shots of one of the Covid-19 vaccines)

Green mutants carrying colossal ray guns,
ridiculous with gray paint and plastic,
Hide beneath the suburban sandpits
of stopped science-fiction time,
Down Gower Street a star-studded block
from Paramount studios,
Waiting to drag down,
with compelling Martian voices,
Gloria Talbot and Carol Ohmart,
who walk by holding hands,
Giggling and hugging,
as they smell the commissary coffee,
Veronica Lake's meat loaf, and
the telescopic screams of Cathy Wilson.
Unearthly moanings now emanate
across the painted picket fences,
Up there, at the end of this hilly painted trail,
where shrill ghostly violins speak madness,
Where ghoulish organ music meshes
with shrieking wind demons,
Poised to catch another human victim;
To gift them with crystals and coma.

COVID GARDENS

Steve McQueen grabs a cheeseburger
with a basket of fries and an egg roll.
Colonel Fielding sits by and warns him,
To avoid certain screen sirens at Republic:
Joan Crawford and Judy Canova, who
Eat his dessert, with a slice of highland green mustang,
and now it is time for the lion to roar,
Time for the marching of everything designed,
to slaughter, annihilate and procreate;
The full United States Army,
backed by violins and the Mitch Miller Gang,
blasting mayhem to the bloated Martians,
Blasting pointed displeasures at him, It,
-mankind developed to its ultimate intelligence-
and his giant sap slaves as they grunt;
Those green, pot-bellied mutants,
galumphing along in the tunnels,
with long metallic zippers and goggles;
The clock keeps ticking;
the explosives are primed.
Time to run, time to wake up David!
Arthur Franz and Hillary Brooke
exchange phone numbers under the table.
They plan to meet later at the Knickerbocker,
for bootleg love a la carte,
Another slippery rendezvous,
on the boulevard of broken dreams.
It is morning still, and
the Times has yet to be read.

STARK HUNTER

Dead stars still haunt
the Paramount commissary;
At midnight
They sit cross-legged with lit cigarettes,
reading their obituaries;
Jimmy Hunt is sitting in the corner,
still wondering what landed
out there, beyond the trees.
The Chordettes are still singing Mister Sandman,
now under the stars at Hollywood Forever.
Each holds a hank of hair
from embalmed beefcake boys,
Rock, Marlon, Steve McQueen
and the brothers Cartwright.
"Wonderful meatloaf, Miss Lake,
Wonderful taste.
You will live forever!"

COVID GARDENS

ANTI-POEM 9
"THE DYING NURSE"

(Poet's Instruction: Пожалуйста, включите «Тихую ночь», читая эту антипоэму.)

A brown '87 Corolla parked on Strub Street
The missus is visiting inside a faded green house
She's nursing a dying yellow nurse at Yule time
She's bringing gifts of unspoken commiseration

Green interior walls argue with green old furniture
Pillows and doilies lie still with a Felix the Cat clock
Stuck on 1957 wallpaper still adhering there ticking
The nurse's daughter opens the green front door
She's a forty-year old career girl with black bangs

Now she is pacing nervously
The carpeted confines of her childhood home
Telling her dying mother to go back to bed now
Telling her to put on a sweater for the cold
Now the green phone rings on the 1957 tea cart
This ivory-skinned daughter wearing Episcopalian shoes
Answers it with legs crossed and head tilted
She is happy to know nurses are coming to sing
Coming to bring a final salute to a dying friend
These angels with sad mittens and hopeful scarves
Coming in a caring caravan to give life back
To the one now perched bravely

STARK HUNTER

High upon the precipice of losing it.

Family pictures in gold frames
Groaning on a television console
A deceased husband in the ground now and
A grown-up daughter wearing ubiquitous green
She stands now by her dying mother
Waiting and watching for a sign of auspicious light
Arm in arm they sway like trees in the wind
The front door opened wide dressed in tinsel

The nurses gather now on the green resigned lawn
Caroling Jingle Bells and birthing magic breath clouds
The dying nurse and her daughter embrace
As Silent Night soars serpentinely above the trees
Like a ghost choir gliding on amniotic carpets
Seeking one last miracle under the starry abyss
The missus and me join in interlocking cold fingers
The dying nurse in tears blows a goodbye kiss

COVID GARDENS

ANTI-POEM 10
"JOHNNY ACE IN HEAVEN"

Big Mama Thornton is singin Ball and Chain
Inside Houston's jumping City Auditorium
It is Christmas 1954 and Johnny Ace is drinking
The hound dog lady has had enough of this game

Suave couples regaled in their funeral best
Sit at moody tables inside the Empire Room
Johnny and Big Mama are pledging their love
Through alcoholic keyholes at the Rice Hotel
The orchestra plays musty blues in the shadows
The long-legged harpist plays without sheet music

Mustached waiters carry black platters of whiskey
To '50's hipsters wearing feathers of peacocks
They dine on caviar corn bread and water cress
Fez-wearing men dressed in white suits belch loudly
Sister Rosetta tunes her Gibson under fake palms
Johnny Ace knows when to turn on the blues charm
Knows when to shred the lowest of the blues bones
There are no secrets behind hotel doors and mirrors
His bride Lois and the kids still wait at the bus depot
But Johnny's going 90 in his Oldsmobile on I-45

"Hey Johnny, sit down and have a drink with me
Bartender, drinks all around especially for my friend
Johnny Ace, the lonely heartsick crooner crushed by love

STARK HUNTER

Johnny, you gambled with death, man, and you lost
Now you sit at the piano by yourself playing a sad blues
And you've been gone so long, Johnny Ace, why? Why?"

The old brass clock still runs at City Auditorium
The Johnny Ace Band is kicking it out again
I'm crazy baby to be in love with you
Fellas with starched cuff links hold their women
Big Mama Thornton is singing Ball and Chain
As the gun is passed to Johnny's shooting hand
"Johnny, it was Christmas
What were you thinking?"

Now I see him again standing at the bar
A suit-wearing crooner looking for love
Drinking shots of vodka and holy water
Tapping his fingers with a wry smile from heaven
"Johnny is that you?
Come all the way from up there to see us?
Truth be told my friend you were crazy that night
Tell us Johnny it ain't so
Tell us you weren't playing the Russian Blues"
"I cross my heart, and if I lie, I hope to die"

COVID GARDENS

ANTI-POEM 11
"SAVOY BROWN AT THE SWING"

Cessna creep.
All destroyed in a heap.
The Swing crashing down in a 1981 fire,
Ghost guitar heroes twanging in a funeral pyre.
The luminous nights of rock and roll mayhem,
Under the Nixon and Kennedy lights straight in,
Xylophone and upright you found my soul,
I can see it as it was when Zappa melted it all,
At the Swing in smoky San Bernardino,
Artist machines jamming nuclear in the old casino,
With echoplex monsters squirming like snakes,
Assaulting the mad Fenders with reverb earthquakes.

(Teeth clenching and rock and roll axes
Grinding and seizing audiences of dreaming stoners
Long-haired wizards passing roach clips to virginal
Hippie girls laden with feathers and Indian beads
Bending over Naugahyde tables reading the horoscopes
Getting banged by tattooed boyfriends in pompadoured
Cadillacs cruising through Whirley's for shrimp and hickies
As lost kids from the duplex hover around the privies
Finding nirvana sandwiches with the roadies out back
Guitars and saxophones make pornos in the afternoon
As dancers from a 1949 musical arrive with decayed garters
They toe the Swing's floor and find it to their liking
The Stones leave wet notes and shuddering guitar solos sizzling

STARK HUNTER

Such rock and roll explosions never heard before
When I met you there in your hippie skirt of zig-zag loom
With turquoise rings and tan Italian legs ready to dance
Kim Simmonds of Savoy Brown was jamming the Boogie
Rocking out like nothing I had ever seen or heard before
And you standing there in the marijuana confines shaking it
You with a joint in hand digging the jumping onslaught)
Cessna creep.
All destroyed in a heap.
At the Swing in smoky San Bernardino.
Artist machines jamming nuclear in the old casino.

(Il est temps pour une pause toilettes maintenant).

COVID GARDENS

ANTI-POEM 12
"THE DREAM PALACE"

Poet's Instruction for the Reader:
(Stop! This can only be read while seated on
your personal toilet in the morning)

Alas, we meet again here in this dream palace,
This restorative oasis of waste finding freedom,
Of wonderful glaciers moving stone granite monuments adrift.
These wondrous healings of saying goodbye to the bad,
Saying adios to lingering used-up remnants of divine fodder.
Now is that wonderful moment in all the epochs of human time!
Of all the grand and glorious moments in the proud annals of life!
Now is the time to let it go!
Let us push and project whatever rockets of love we can fly!
We do this in the names of our mothers.
We do this because our walking taxicabs require it.
Push! Push!
Wonderful! We did it!
Alas, until we meet again here in this dream palace,
I say, ce qui entre, doit sortir.

Oh, I see you are still here in this dream palace,
Seeking the holy grail of beautiful divine migrations,
Of lovely caravans with rich traders dressed in gems,
Flashing by like rivers of fire into this sea of frustrations,
Of legendary expeditions emerging from sunless jungles.
Push darling! Think of hamburgers and shakes in a dark car,

STARK HUNTER

Imagine endless currents of moving solid earth and raging rivers,
Visualize eating two ripe apples with a glass of God's own milk!
Good!
Remember, we do this in the names of our mothers.
Wonderful!
Push darling, your bodily salvation has arrived!
May your beatified baggage be whisked away finally,
Into a watery eternity, of swishes and magical flushes!
You did it as it was your destiny to do it.
Alas! Ce qui entre, doit sortir.
("These helpful walls know the usual sounds and smells,
But they remain green and pink, and they don't complain.")

COVID GARDENS

ANTI-POEM 13
"EXPERIMENT FOR TWO MOUTHS AND ONE EAR"

(Poet's Instruction: This anti-poem rhymes. A big sin.
Say a penance of two prayers, your choice, to God asking
for forgiveness, after reading this rhyming anti-poem)

There is a strange droning animal-sound in the high air
Like eight-legged sopranos searching for a place to snare
The wind-chimes in my green yard tinkle its evening prayer
For they do not belong to any real love song or refrain
Nor to anything or anyone with half a heart or brain
Those unending trudging footsteps forward never reaching
Never finding the blinding soul visions of a faraway teaching
A profoundly restful spot distant under the stars superfluous
You and I are there clenched tight as the wind softly touches us
Caresses us, with tender entreaties in our piercing aroused cries
There is a sensational sunset hiding in the temple of your eyes
I look deeply into them as you quiver with free-fall emotions
As you slide into easy love with my denials of fear so unspoken
Like an enchanted rain falling comatose on dark hillsides at noon
We embrace in the misting rain as night slits its brow with sad June

(You need to pray now…)

STARK HUNTER

ANTI-POEM 14
"HEADLESS JESUS"

(Poet's Instruction: Please eat one slice of pizza
while reading this anti-poem)

the toxic pulsing streams
of sudsy milk bone retardations
alas finds nothing worth reading
in this stultifying void of the insipid

though now we can see
the soul-dead zombie hoards
milking the hardened hillsides
sucking down adrenal cocktails
with ripe cherries at last impaled
shot into the heart of the thing
by the pliant stick of a pizza tree
held aloft by robed Finns and Them
the dusty denizens of Gard du Mord.

'oh these Parisian ghosts
maybe they ought to unlock the church doors
open the bone drawers beneath the niter
now for an excursion
into the big nave –
studded with paints and statues "passez!!
"todos estos rostros sagrados que no hablan"

COVID GARDENS

now we see it
amongst all these desecrations
the headless Jesus
once again tortured and killed
by the death-masters and their moronic Igors

"C'est le fou qui dit qu'il n'y a pas de dieu"

STARK HUNTER

ANTI-POEM 15
"DANCING CHEEK TO CHEEK"

(Poet's Instruction: Forestil dig at danse med nogen, du ikke kender).

Never mind the Bon Ami.
These resplendent floors have
A shine all their own.
Like red butch wax
Slicking up a brown cowlick.

I can see the ghost girls again,
Dancing cheek to cheek,
To Sue Thompson's 'Norman,'
Inside a 1962 malted milk dive,
On the outskirts of shady Pacoima.
I see the smoking cool boys basking
In dude blue appointments,
Ambling like fish kings down
Neon-blasting Van Nuys Boulevard,
Strutting and striding
With determined appendages,
Belting out syncopated screams,
Into the jiving bebop nights,
Ella, Billie and Blossom,
Bellowing forth their manacled anthems.

Never mind the Bardahl or
the Oxydol connivings.

COVID GARDENS

We state with firm fingers
Our trust in Swanson TV dinners;
Our dedication with bated teeth
To the gods of tin foil;
We embrace their vaunted creeds,
Their dry dispositions.
We openly endorse their tasty ego trips,
Dripping in jazz,
Dripping in fried blues and rhythm,
With diva-chicks lacquered up,
Like old cut-outs from torn magazines,
Buried under cracked cellophane.

We can see the grey looming shadows,
Of our dead friends dancing out there,
Not talking, not breathing, not looking.
Our old friends swinging at the Aragon,
Gogi Grant and Helen Humes,
Jodie Sands and Gale Storm;
All looking for cocaine and weed,
Crossing over now into our wicked scene;
Now in this death garden,
May we have a suave serenade,
By the lovely Norma Zimmer?

Never mind the fog creeping in,
Traipsing unseen over the murky back bay.
We have our troubadours here
Wearing fedoras and black shades.
Old songs once sung by dead men,

STARK HUNTER

Are tonight being sweetly sung again;
Sarah Vaughn and Hazel Scott,
Rise from caskets brimming with the blues.
Glasses filled with beer suds and addictions,
Find singing lips and white flashing teeth,
Striding on stage holding tattooed carnations.
The ghost girls are dancing naked now,
Cheek to cheek mired in neon whispers;
Penetrations and encumbrances ensue
Magically, atop the waxed dance floor.

COVID GARDENS

ANTI-POEM 16
"QUARANTINED"

(Poet's instruction: Because of Covid-19 health protocols, kindly wear an N95 mask while reading this anti-poem)

Waking up to this strange dream
First sight is the checkered ceiling
Then the antique bathroom mirror
I see old age and worried red eyes
I see another drawn day of breathing
My beard is out of control with grey
I am home now and not going out
I hear helicopters often in the sky
The morning time is escape time
The missus and me watch another one
Another end-of-the-world imitation
Just like ice milk; not the real thing
We sit and netflix the hours like sharks
Devouring phony time with no incisors
As with a glass vase holding heartbeats
We know dinner time is the best time
As another anxious nothing day slinks by
There will be kitchen trips for comforts
There will be basement sojourns for spirits
But no afternoon excursions to the shops
No possibility of even meeting stone statues
Inside this wooden box is where we must hide
Out of this window is as far as I can see

STARK HUNTER

Listen
There is hopeful music in the distant rooms
There are praying voices behind the closed doors

COVID GARDENS

ANTI-POEM 17
"LIVING IN A NETFLIX MOVIE"

(Poet's Instruction: Binge-Soma anti-poem
hii mara tano kwa siku kwa wiki)

This world of trees and milkshakes made of styrofoam,
Is reeling like a sad drunkard trying to find his way home.
He is mad with worry as the monsters in the brush growl,
There is something lurking in the dark and begins to howl.
Something foul with teeth that loves its flesh to be chewy,
We are all caught and hopelessly living in a Netflix movie.

This town of roads and bridges with cheeseburgers dangling,
Is fraught with shadows foaming into blobs for the mangling,
Townsfolk run for the sheriff who is crazed with reptile eyes,
The mayor and the widow are caught naked in a bed of lies.
Something is wrong here in this oasis of corruption and duty,
We are all caught and hopelessly living in a Netflix movie.

This street of shaded houses and tinted sedans sleeps at midnight,
As hoards of spider dogs come out of the sewers clenched to bite,
Into sleeping bedrooms they slink with bloody fangs dripping,
Onto the necks of terrified girls their hairy tongues go licking,
Something dead inside the attic is waiting to attack come Tuesday,
We are all caught and hopelessly living in a Netflix movie.

This room of cobwebbed curtains and a dire bed made of disease,
Lies in silent refrain with the choirs of fear singing hymns to Louise.

STARK HUNTER

Just another victim of the silent killing thing hidden in the TV forest,
A man-eating microbe with hungry teeth looking for a pretty florist,
But something foul and green is growling loudly from below, truly,
We are all caught and hopelessly living in a Netflix movie.

COVID GARDENS

ANTI-POEM 18
"HIERONYMUS BOSCH WAKES UP"

(Poet's Instruction: Beware. This poem is disturbing.
Reading it may cause mental and spiritual distress.
Proceed with caution. Rated R).

Toxic slime girls slink out of the muck looking for man-worms,
Hidden under blue plastic tarps,
they forage like piranhas with nose rings,
Devouring cosmic meats carved from rat corpses dead in the fields.
The marching villagers step over bossa nova-bodies
quivering in tinted mud.
Hieronymus Bosch wakes up from his Garden of Earthly Delights.

He sees his visions while eating tortured donuts made of mendicancy.
Scorpion drones find the fleeing ones in old churches, skinning
With razor fingers their flesh from head to toe as they scream,
Guttural whippings with rivers of erupting bowel retchings.
Hieronymus Bosch wakes up from his Garden of Earthly Delights.

Time now to find a clever moment to relax with this fine meal,
Of beating hearts and slithering tongues in tangy stomach bile.
Monster machines dressed as humans secretly probe the still places,
The quiet carnivorous places,
smelling for a living victim trussed and tied.
Hieronymus Bosch wakes up from his Garden of Earthly Delights.

Gangrene girls wearing dirty bandages do their enchilada pole dances,

STARK HUNTER

Singing karaoke with flying haunches stewed in bloody meat sauces,
The guys with Hamiltons stand and holler
as zombie killers lacerate from behind,
Removing dead astonished stares from severed heads
bathed in tomato soup.
Hieronymus Bosch wakes up from his Garden of Earthly Delights.

He samples the various delicacies served on icy trays by priestly ghouls,
Sacrificed torso-meats branded by fiery pokers
as giant wasp creatures sting,
Slash and eviscerate coeds inside crushed cars beneath melting buildings,
Avalanching to the churning cheese-pit of sulphur fire
and dead men's bones.
Hieronymus Bosch wakes up from his Garden of Earthly Delights.

Giant crawling eyes slither out of the New York subways
grabbing young prey;
Screaming girls dressed in tight skirts run blindly
into the pulling sucking tentacles,
As the crawling eating eyes burp out gnarled flesh and bones
as they slink by;
Bloodshot stoned eyeballs drag whimpering girls
to eating nests underground.
Hieronymus Bosch wakes up from his Garden of Earthly Delights.

Invisible T-Rex from the nether regions of virus paperbacks
and tin lunch boxes,
Arises again to find another fainting coed and carries her to the sea cliffs.
It finds dead dudes living their final moments
before the teeth and the grinding;

COVID GARDENS

Men's arms and legs dangle as the floor sucks downward
with inward-turning gears.
Hieronymus Bosch wakes up from his Garden of Earthly Delights.

A new morning emerges
with the opening of barred doors and cellar windows.
The girls choir practice proceeds
with sunlit unguents sung wistfully in Latin refrains;
Dead corpses dressed in green and purple
rise from their graves smoking cigarettes.
They take cherry cough drops
sprinkled with lemon sneezes and endorphin squeezes.
Hieronymus Bosch falls asleep again in his Garden of Earthly Delights.

STARK HUNTER

ANTI-POEM 19
"SOMETHING LURKING IN CLAPHAM COMMON"

(Poet's Instruction: Cette instruction n'est pas à suivre si elle est rédigée en français)

Ah Sir, if you please!
I believe there is something rotten,
Dripping lugubriously upon your broad lapel.
Sir, let me put some water to it
Spiffy-like, as they say, and pronto.
I dare say, sir, before it stains indelibly,
As with the fast horses at Ascot;
They move swiftly, as we must now, sir,
And ascertain most assuredly that,
There is something oozing up in the sky,
For this rotten dripping is splashing my eyes,
And my overshoes are sloshing like beagles
In the snow; but now the back door is ajar for
The milkman; see, he brings the butter from afar.
But now it seems, there is something else coming,
Something infinitesimal,
Lurking, as they say in Clapham Common;
Something on the hind leg of the green spittle bug;
As with the fast horses at Ascot;
This monster of mucus can slide by unbeknownst,
Like a current of wet membrane air,
Finding astonished souls walking by with hat and cane.
I dare say, sir, we must stay here and not stir.

COVID GARDENS

We must sit and drink tea with seedless lemon slices,
You and I, and the lovely Mrs. Macmurdo.
She, with the fox fur and the dark-gartered nylons;
We can dally here awhile with downcast stares,
Imagining the worst, as we sip this tonic of fear. Or
We can defy the elements, and gladly enjoin here.
Ah Sir, if you please!
Have you a light for this unsteady hand?

STARK HUNTER

ANTI-POEM 20
"SNIFFING A CORONER'S VAN"

(Poet's Instruction: Bhema kancane ugwayi
ngenkathi ufunda le anti-poem).

Sniffing a coroner's van parked
under the overhang.
I smell something dead inside,
I smell a sad funeral in the near offing.

He lived next door for a few years
Smoking cigarettes all the time.
She was a Cuban mother of two,
Divorced and estranged from Big Louie,
Who beat her on occasion in the 90's.
The passing years pierced Lena's heart
Like a pick axe into hard mud.

The arrival of silver-haired Neil,
Chain smoking and driving a Chrysler,
Brought forth the odors of interminable
Cigarette smoke and car exhaust,
Enough to know when his tall willowy soul was
Present in his blue backyard,
Sitting at a blue table
By a blue swimming pool;
There Neil smoked and lived,
Lived for ten trips around the big campfire

COVID GARDENS

In the banal night up there.
Lived and coughed and spat as the passing decade
Wheezed on by like hurt cats running from a fire.

Every day at 4 o'clock
Tall Neil stood stooped behind the Chrysler,
Peering into his trunk,
Looking, examining, studying something inside there;
Not sure what; maybe his collection
Of dog-eared maps, or letters prized and
Well-read from old loves written in cursive swirls
With bright pink ink, redolent of an archaic perfume.
Maybe as he stood there he was
Counting cigarette cartons, every single nail,
Assuring himself all will be well.
For the time being.

I miss seeing the silver-haired Neil,
Standing outside there behind his car.
I often wonder how he did, you know,
Dying inside his house like he did,
A few fleeting years back, when he was
Laid out on a hospital bed In Lena's living room,
An oxygen tank pumping air like a crazed oil derrick.
I wonder if Neil died like my father,
Lying there and slowly drowning,
Without being in the water.

Sniffing a coroner's van parked under the overhang.
I smell something that was once alive,

STARK HUNTER

tall and silver-haired, lying hidden in there.
Tall Neil is stooped over looking at his maps.

COVID GARDENS

ANTI-POEM 21
"THE BAMBINO"

(Poet's Instruction: Softly play
"Lovable And Sweet" by Annette Henshaw).

If we can all just Lindbergh this thing through baby
Just keep going for 33 hours non-stop on this hard floor
Maybe you and me can go stepping out jazz style later
Find a nearby watering hole serving memory love bombs
Listen to a few belted-out marshmallow meltdowns
Sung by Miss Annette whose too scared to sing the fast ones

Lovable and Sweet are her throbbing trombones with
Dancing nomads finding their currency in the be bops
The hot dog boys in suspenders shag a few from the Bambino
Sing up sing fast Miss Hanshaw with the Five behind you
Sam and Lou dance dizzy boy circles in the cadenced wings

Miss Annette sings to her daddy dear to please come home
The world wags through the neon streets with ambush music
Now Miff and Benny mouth the spit rhythms under mean reeds
Don't treat me cold daddy please the Bambino points to center

Irish Al Smith downs a cold one in catholic solitude at Chumley's
His wife wants him home now but he's listening to Miss Annette
She's crooning If you want the Rainbow You Must Have the Rain

He's recalling youthful days and frolics as the dance floor lights up

STARK HUNTER

Then deep drums of defeat provide bombshell pillows of rum
The Bambino hits one into River Avenue sharkskin gangsters
Arrive in steel-plated Duesenbergs with high-heeled backfisch

Now ladies and gentlemen, step forward for our next dance delight
Tell them children how it is gentlemen strike it up now as we pivot
As we twirl our knees with sweaty chains and hidden liquor flasks

"Sweetheart baby I love you but I'm afraid you don't love me"

Here she is the grand and glorious Annette Hanshaw,
The happy girl The perky girl
The one-room Manhattan gal at the end of her rope
Madly in love with the men she adores who refuse to love her back
Torturing her with empty debonair squeezes under a shady cocktail
Their touching heart-pounding jive movements in loveless cuff-links
Annette's sweet men they who absconded in never-sleeping 1928
Her innocent kisses her tilted breasts finding their seashell buttons

Now the forgetting begins the slaughter of heartsick compasses
As another song is offered up Miss Annette dreads the moment
Dreads the cough that may come, fears the night as other voices
Cheer the Bambino as he rounds third in the American jive joint

"That's all."

COVID GARDENS

ANTI-POEM 22
"JOHNNY RAY TIPTOES"

(Poet's instruction: Play Johnny Ray, singing
"Walking My Baby Back Home").

A post-war Gotham drizzle descends downward like rice stones
Lashing the bleeding ashes of Julius, Ethel and Sam Sheppard
They sit drinking tequila sunrises under death's closed umbrella
The lonely gentleman from Wisconsin flicks ashes at Radio City
As the white-legged Rockettes finish their asphalt war dance

Now Johnny Ray tiptoes on stage wearing loose black corduroy
He holds his ear and serenades to the screams of the rapturous
His hidden hearing-aide buzzing the rhythms of wooden ambivalence
His secret lover doesn't need a restful chin or a sad crying song
As they make rabid love at the Copa with the Journal American
Peeping through 10 point typeset his smooth rehearsed anthems
His crescendoing climb through H-bomb appetizers and quinine

Now he's walking his baby back home under the weeping stars
The taxicabs whir by like mad yellow bugs sniffing old tuna fish
There it is the famous four-story brownstone at East 68th Street
The ghostly doorman still stands bowing to the quietly desperate
Still opens the door crack for Johnny and Dorothy to sneak inside

(Post Poem WordScape):

(Bennett Cerf offers a confused toast with

STARK HUNTER

cathode ray remonstrances.
Try drinking it now.
Johnny Ray Electric launches into it
The little white cloud that cried
These partisans here and these weepers
They release ball-bearing heart collisions
I cannot stand it I cannot bear it any longer)

COVID GARDENS

ANTI-POEM 23
"THE IT"

(Poet's Instruction: Softly play
"Cow Cow Boogie" by Ella Mae Morse).

Oh! I am trapped in this spinning spool
Trapped and tied like scared firewood
Bundled and flayed like tired granite
The termite men come to sniff the stones
I wonder if they need my help to find It
To coax It out from its present darkness
To say Hey, we are your friends here
We say welcome to our earth garden
Where the sinsemilla flirt with the dandy-lions

We say bienvenidos to my living friends
And we say bienvenu to all my dead ones
Strike up the band! It is time for music now
Time to stroll arm in arm through these gardens
Hear the strums of this Mexican ghost guitar as
The señorita girls ascend the trees like lizards
Dressed in the hues of sunset resplendence

It is time now, my friends! Time for closed eyes
Time to slink behind this tree for extreme kisses
Wet and passionate as ripe cherries in a dish
You and the dark princess wearing red lipstick
Seventeen years passed with brunet tresses kneeling

STARK HUNTER

"Entra en el blues y la princesa boogie
De hace mucho tiempo llevando su corazón"
And now ladies and gentlemen, "tis time for
Ella Mae Morse and Freddie Slack on keys with
Cow Cow Boogie scratching the floor's eyes out
Singing his cow cow boogie in the strangest way.
" Comma ti yi yi yeah Comma ti yippity yi yeah"

I wonder what musty creepy place this is
The pathways here mumble people's names aloud
Names long ago absorbed into this seeping bower
Where all my dead friends sleep in soft tombs
Singing the muted songs of whimpering heartbeats
Drenched in mercury dime lavender and aerosols

Oh! I am tied and cannot escape these termites
These gnawing wall cracks of time and temerity
Shh! Who is that coming down the shrouded path
Coming with wriggling fish sticks and band-aides
The cowboy boogie half-breed is eating the weed
Senor! My friend! We have been expecting you
This is your chair, and this is your bed hombre!
Oh, my friend, we have much to say to each other
There is time now to sit and rest and ponder the It
We continue to look and search for It in this rubble
Of taco plates brimming with beans and certitudes
They eat the crumbs of the giver and taker of all
I wonder if they need my help to find It nowhere
Find the bric-a-brac of cedar-smelling do-nothings
This side of death's last excursion to the perfumed loo

COVID GARDENS

A half mile down this hairy hallway of flailing arms

Hey my friend!
Did you get the beer and the bread at the A & P
Did you rescue your babbling kid by the bric-a-brac
Hey, man I have a big surprise for you
These ripe bananas of white pearl unpeeled

Get on board
Little children get on board little children
Get on board little children
There's room for many or more

STARK HUNTER

ANTI-POEM 24
"RIDING SUBURBAN SHOTGUN"

(Poet's instruction: Kindly play softly in the background,
"Spill the Wine" by Eric Burdon and War)

Are you ready for this summer cruise
This surreal sojourn to the asphalt waffle iron
Are you prepared to ride suburban shotgun
Singing loud from Pickering to Bob 's Big Boy
Dissecting Whittier Boulevard like red
Mag-wheeled beetles in the dead debris
We will chase hormonal daydreams
Wearing D cup righteousness in night-glow
We will spend late hours eating electric water
From the same cup of green ethereal desire

A thousand glaring headlights of our dream
Caravan drawing up with drivers braking
Turning now with Burdon slurping singing
Spill the Wine amidst 1970 night-smog noises
Back to the boulevard never ending ceasing
These endless u-turns looking for heaven scents
Cruiser chicks in lipstick halters flipping off boys
From purple machine-gunned one night stands
Of summer couch squeezings and purring zippers
Sleeping half-dressed during Johnny's monologue

Now War wails again the ancient refrain

COVID GARDENS

Spill the wine, Dig that girl
Now she guides my fingers to the well of voices
Perfumed street lights stand blindfolded but recall
September nights long ago in the groping Impala
Those bell-bottomed flirtations transmigrating under
Neil Young's stars there we ascended Sugar Mountain
As young fish jump from the spires to the cold gushings
We finger-started the jumping mind-birds to ride there
To glide there in the black light illuminations before us

STARK HUNTER

ANTI-POEM 25
"WATERING THE GRASS"

Watering the grass with this long rubbery snake-thing
Squirting hydrogen essences into the rainbow wavelengths
Arousing the life atoms
This birthing of free chemicals in flux

I need for this small ocean painting to be green
in all its tides and turnings
I need the bird of paradise
to gawk upon these silent maneuvers
I hear female voices in the distance
coming from the lemon grove
Under sky-filled canopies
of green leaf artistry they stand huddled
Chanting full-sun madrigals
within hedges of green-eyed aromas
I need the ensuings of the dichondra bells
behind walls of wisteria

Fragments
Of your daily mirror image
Let loose upon these plastic voicings
Can you hear the snide ones
Speaking to the creeping charlies with gaping teeth
They offer nothing except
Another drink in the golden rum darkness
With miss lonely heart weeping chasers

COVID GARDENS

Mixing strapless suds with lipstick hysteria
Careful there
She will fry your brains with peanuts and lost stares
There will be nothing left to say to each other   again
There will be prolonged silences
As she sits pondering nothing
I will look again at the cosmetics applied and
I will pretend I'm in love

"Ohh, waking up next to you every morning
In this squeaking deathbed to be
Really man, is there no better bed than this
Might we find a spare one
There in your pantry amongst the brooms
Approximately where your dead mother cooked"

Time for me to be going honey,
but wait
We are not yet done turning this ancient screw
The grovelers outside drivel like idiot dogs
They lie in wait for my blood-dabbed toenails

    (Poet's instruction at this point in reading this Anti-Poem:
    Kindly stop reading and close your eyes. Imagine being
    with someone alone in a vast field of shade trees.
    After one minute continue reading poem)

Shhh be quiet Over there is the gate to the meadow
You and I must enter our steadfast embraces there
Penetrate the barriers to our wild-eyed encroachments

STARK HUNTER

I accept your piercing breasts as gifts to be savored
As with the sweet flowers of summer's grand heat
They forever bend to the begging discourses of the wind
They listen only when uttered words need full alliteration
These trees go forever to the west where my past winks
Remembering those times better than my desire to forget
Here, hold my hand as we step upon these veins of Eden
Your toddling footsteps answering mine with invisible signals
Now the insistent wind leads us to the comfortable shadows

Time to water the lawn again
Time to calculate nothing here
Time to go upstairs again
Time for eternal satin interludes
Of rare earth vicissitudes
Time to dance wild-eyed now
Time to water the grass again
With this long rubbery snake-thing

COVID GARDENS

ANTI-POEM 26
"EMPTY CHAIR"

(Poet's Instructions: בקר את החולים. התפלל למתים)

Musty hallway
Mourning shadows
Vacant bed
Rosary beads
Cold candles
Still shoes
Hairy brush
Dog-eared bible
Vacuumed rug
Potted flowers
Open window
Empty chair
Pale mirror
Hooked coat
Family portrait
Lost sock
Hushed room
Unplugged lamp
Forgotten thimble
Feathered hat
Clock ticking
Cat purring
Perfume bottle
Diamond ring

STARK HUNTER

Lace doily
Empty chair
Mouse skittering
Torn nylons
Hidden Ruger
Locked suitcase
Stainless bedpan
Crucifix walls
Drooping ferns
Silent bell
Empty chair
Locked wheelchair
Death polaroid
Ivory combs
Black-book hidden
Cigarette holder
Eyelashes fake
Ransacked purse
Silver dollar
Compact gauze
Funeral receipt
Empty chair

COVID GARDENS

ANTI-POEM 27
"MOSQUITO MUSIC"

(Poet's instruction to reader: Moderately play
"Stranger on the Shore" by Acker Bilk, 1962 recording)

Mosquito music
I pound my drum for you
Bare my expressive soul
Strip my ego restraints
All for you as you pose there
You say your name is Hortense
I am Wilfred
Do you believe me?
Do I believe you?
Waiter!
A white whale for the lady!

Your advertisement flexes well
Pursed moist lips shadow-puckering
Unctuous red eyes pleading for
More morning calisthenics in rhymes
Am seeing something shiny there

More mosquito music?
Ah, Stranger on the Shore
That clarinet is a dark woman
Like you ambling under garden strobes
She with the endlessly long legs

STARK HUNTER

Glistening with twilight cold cream
Sauntering over skirted black holes

I wonder if we might stop here
Stop to imagine this leafy molting
This incredible collision of knees
I drink to your nestling mountains
To your soft iridescent battlements

Come inside now
The door is unlocked
Here you will see excellent things
Paintings hanging on listening walls
Listening with forlorn longings
Dark halter-strap disengagings
Mouth pressings and swishings
Mysteriously happen here
As with silences under a tilted moon

Now she comes this way
Comes to call with vinyl records
Old albums of Beethoven and Bilk
That incredible cool clarinet
The irresistible embraces of memory
Talking privately in the distant gardens
Kissing the suave wind ghosts there
You walk ahead now flashing gams
Posing for eyes that never see you

Mosquito music

COVID GARDENS

I pound my drum for you
Bare my expressive soul
Leave my male thing on the table
All for you
As you wallow in freshly-eaten footsteps
There in front of me now
Dancing to mosquito music

STARK HUNTER

ANTI-POEM 28
"APACHE"

(Poet's Instruction: Softly play "Apache"
by Jorgen Ingmann, 1961)

Olathe and Yamka
Cochise and
Mescalero
Varlebena - forever
Ya'ateh – Hello to
These streaming flower gardens
These feathered priests of Gaan
Their white flags of truce burning

Geronimo
You can fly now
Fly as an osprey conquering
Retaking the cottonwoods of Tubac
Feasting on rabbit and mourning dove
Drop seed grass and agave blossom
Hating the white lies the soft knives

Mangas
You are the blood warrior in the stars
Brave as the wind pinned to the sky
T`Inde, Inde, N`dee, N`ne
Your children still sing the old songs
Voicing the call of the spirit dancers

COVID GARDENS

The crown dancers of Pinos Altos
Lipan and Salinero

Gaan is pointing now
East west north and south
To Cookes Canyon and
The Florida Mountains
Your sleeping villages
Dream again the heartbreak
Of Dragoon Springs
Humility's white flag hoisted
With Mangas' head
Boiled for the white owls
Dangling with lizard tongues
The atrocities of Adobe Wells
Visiting upon the noble innocents
We can hear them again the
Apache choirs of the dead
Screaming into the savage night
The high mountain spirits forever
Bringing dreams of sky-blue light
The streaming peaceful flower gardens
T`Inde, Inde, N`dee, N`ne

STARK HUNTER

ANTI-POEM 29
"APOCALYPTIC SINATRA"

(Poet's Instruction: Basahin lamang ang tulang
ito sa katapusan ng mundo).

We now hear the low-moaning monster music of Akira
Drums rolling like battalions of running earth beasts
The city convulsing in dread of the hideous fang thing
Presently emerging from the belching retching sea
An 8-legged brain-eater with purple-thorned suckers
Big as a cloud plucking toweled sexy blondes screaming
High into its toothy ripping beak tied by fleshy hooks
Screaming wildly to the last as pleas for help find no response

"Oh honey you look fine tonight in that peeling plaid skirt
Get in sweetie and let me take you to Ted's Super Burger
There we will gather in the french-fried mustard shade
We will play the music of Akira loudly under this shy moon
Make cinematic love in the backseat of this American horror story"
But now the sirens blare forth as the sucking monster approaches
Oozing omnipresently into the sewers of showering brunettes
Grabbing naked ankles as Sinatra croons on a distant record player
"All or nothing at all half a love never appealed to me"

"Let us bring the shovels and the picks when all is contained
Let us call for the army, the air force and the marines
Let us set up this cigar stand first and don't forget the marmalade"
"My heart wants you Steve Martin I want to marry you and be your wife

COVID GARDENS

Make love to me Steve as if there are no more tomorrows"
Then with tentacled annihilation she is schlepped away screaming
Into the gaseous bowels of something indescribable and horrendous
"c'est ma danse"

At prayer for the city in silent bowed repose kneel the redheads
On petition pads made of lilac and Frankincense burgers al la vera
They look upward to their sweet heaven with tilted mouths salivating
Wearing plaid beanies in homage to the virgin girls of Saint Bernadette
Frankenstein zombies outside smell young flesh breaking down the doors
Giving chase to the nubile ones cowering in the concealed recesses
Dragged away now like shivering catfish awaiting the midday butchering
Father Fitzpatrick in black skullcap blesses the dead as they slide by

Whimpering like porn puppies hungry for dishes served by donkeys
Children lovers lock the doors behind them as they receive absolutions
Prophylactic dinosaur men deliver the afterthought of something wicked
Finding wet towels smeared in talcum sweat and lipstick stains
Peering mindlessly into fake two-way mirrors of chrome ecstasy
Ablaze inside a creepy mansion of old plumbing and locked rooms with
Erotic shadows dancing on the ceiling
as sucking purple tentacles slink by
"Sinatra is the best, the best oh Steve Steve make love to me baby"
"And if I fell, fell under the spell of your call
Don't you know I would be caught in the undertow…"

We again hear the low-moaning monster music of Akira
Bringing in the devastation of Tokyo with strident strings
And now the army the air force and the marines enter in
Saving the devastated and the dying as rice rockets pounce

STARK HUNTER

Destroying the hideous fang thing with pink acid bombs
Sending it to an artificial hell only the casting director knows about
"That's a wrap for today folks Steve got a minute I need a word"
Limousines driven by headless chauffeurs drive inside the studio
Red spurting blood erupt like geysers from open necks to the sky
These plasma fountains of rose flower gravy flooding the streets
"Run for your lives!"

Sinatra is singing now in the smoky distance under a hazy street light
Dead women corpses stride by wearing reeking furs and feathered hats
Sucking on cigarette holders
with Constance DeMille and Ethel Rosenberg
"Hey, s'il te plaît, n'approche pas tes lèvres de ma joue
Ne souris pas ou je serai perdu au-delà de mes souvenirs"

COVID GARDENS

ANTI-POEM 30
"THE MURMAIDS"

(Poet's Instruction: Play softly, "Popsicles and Icicles" twice,
by the Murmaids, 1963, while reading this Anti-Poem)

AA
(the sick grandmother
scrounges in her squeaky wheelchair
pounding the glass window meekly
from within her yellow-walled bedroom
pounding with weak hands and
stroke-infested arms
old english arms with black splotches
and smeared-on eucalyptus rub
pounding and thumping old glass
as the boys outside dance and dribble
a voit basketball inscribed by Cousy
afoot the hot pavement in the setting sun
pete lucero takes his black pointed shoes off
as he shoots dream baskets from heaven
right before our eyes standing there in 1963
with the wind blowing through his hair
dave gregg and steve hope pass the ball
to paul moore and jim buckholtz,
the old hoop atop the garage jangling again
as the sick grandmother sits silent
behind her dark window pondering
the avocado stars)

STARK HUNTER

BB
The Murmaids lay it out singing of the boys they love
Singing like three perfect clocks micro-synchronized
Sitting now for a quick black and white at the ivories
There's Sally, Carol and Terry sipping teenage cocktails
Making small talk and giggling at what's coming soon
Coming like mad pilgrims from the old demarcations
Arriving in waistcoats aboard atonal boats with wings
Something hairy with four heads shouting at the girls
Something musical about everyone needing to be in love
These teenage murmaids in bangs giggle now at the boys
Who lug guitars and amps at midnight like battle-axes
Waiting to wage sound assaults upon the groveling

CC
Time now to slip through these sneezing two-by-fours
Time to jump headlong into the air and stay there
To jump back in time to a quiet 1964
A Friday night at the drive-in
In that cold gray time at the Sundown on Washington
A bleak funeral season with old Baba in the ground
Newly birthed by death in the catholic graveyard
And Kennedy is gone too and buried deep in snow
With April and Nino serenading him from a Lincoln

DD
Now the Murmaids take to the airwaves singing merrily
"Popsicles Icicles wind blowing through his hair…"
You and I are kissing wildly inside a 1963 beige Impala
Parked on ancient asphalt next to the bending oleanders

COVID GARDENS

Dressed in loose Levis with a guitar cradling in your arms
I unbuttoned your entire life with a toothpick
Kennedy's astonished corpse must be shivering now as the days
Shuffle past these restless winter yawns at dark dusk
Looming ahead a dead road sign made of glass straw
Buried inside a coffin cloud

EE
(Riding in this cold funeral limousine sitting
Next to living people wearing black clothes
Sunny and the Sunglows sing inside my mind
As the black hearse leaves the stained church
With black cross-eyed motorcycles leading the way
No conversations heard or uttered as time stops
I remember the eleven year old boy sitting there
He was wearing black shoes for his first death ride)

FF
The Murmaids again sing Popsicles and Icicles
Perfectly inside his perplexed imperfect mind as
The hearse turns into silent Calvary Cemetery
Drives to the open hole yawning on avenue B
Father Elliot blesses the body wearing black shades
And now he has said his words and made the Sign
With guarded assessments he walks back to his impala
Swishing the September dust from his laundered stole
This new hole filled now with english arms and hands
Its tiny denizens searching for her embalmed allegiances
Ready to get busy with the new curtains and the towels
Ready for the feasting and the flaying of the new meats

STARK HUNTER

Tasting a late summer barbecue under the avocado stars

———————

(Poet's after-note: Pay these girls. It has been over half a century.)

COVID GARDENS

ANTI-POEM 31
"ILLINOIS"

(Poet's instruction: Play "Harlem Nocturne" by Illinois Jacquet, in the background, while reading this anti-poem)

Driving in now are the cool cats in Hudson chrome
Listening to "Illinois" play the Nocturne in a blue dream,
Listening to a master blow his sax like nothing heard before
He sidles up to you with that thing and you are gone, man!
Gone from this crazy world to something mysterious and cool
"You look dreamy tonight, honey. Your beauty is like that sax
Steamy and mysterious with plenty of secrets to be found
May I put my arm around you, here at this lonely table?
May I reach over and kiss you in this candle-lit kaleidoscope?"

Sedately walking my lady now down this neon boulevard
Smelling fast cigars and perfumed saxophone love-making
The noir lights blink and hum in this drunk insect hide-away
Cool riding gents with silver-chained time pieces dangling
Sip whiskey-sours cavorting with the lonely-hearts in nylons
She puts her head on his shoulder now as they sway there
Float there on the ballroom floor at the Rice Hotel in Houston
The two of them finding convenient steps to the Skylight
Necking after midnight in this hazy Art Deco dreamscape

(I hear "Illinois" raising his voice over there. He just a kid)
"Calm down, boy,"
"Want to hear my sax, or not?"

STARK HUNTER

(Dudes and chicks lining up outside the Empire Room
Smelling lilac cologne and forever chomping at the bit
Ready now to dance the aroused night into a jazzy coma
A numbing cool dance leading to nowhere in particular)
"Yeah, man. Those out there want to hear your sad sax"
"Then, we all come in through the front door, right?"

The undertakers by now have come for them all
As the locusts of the lowlands have come for it all
Our fancy-free friends from 1938 are buried now
Under fabulous blades of tall grass they securely sleep
The cigarette girl, and her rich boss Mister Jones plus
All the guys in the band, Milton, Arnette and Wild Bill
Maxie the bouncing bartender, and all the powder girls
They are the undead now, the smiling unbreathing ones
Sipping forgotten cocktails with regretful smoke hovering
Arrayed still in their burial best, black suit and top hat
Classic dead men sitting and smoking old Cuban stogies
As they tenderly caress the dainty fingers of their dead wives
"Illinois" plays the Harlem Nocturne with his pale shadowy friends
"Easy boys, easy. Play it like your heart's beating again. Easy"

COVID GARDENS

ANTI-POEM 32
"PULSING HUMANS"

(Poet's Instruction: 艺术本质上是纯净的。请不要试图理解这首诗)

A wine-dark sunset slowly caresses the shivering west
As drooling dogs unleashed roam the hollowed grounds
Burying divergent bones with an urgent sniveling swagger
Houses of brick and pebble dash stand in a mordant light
Pulsing humans rush about from house to shadowy house
Room to blistering room with pearls and chocolate cameras
Midnight rendezvous girls lock their doors putting on lipstick
Their perfumed necks drip with clasping stars and metal dreams
They enter in through the back door in tandem eye caresses
These two drooling dogs with pulling incisors thrusting sideways
Mother and father lie sleeping upstairs numb to the naughty hours
The perspiring sneaking hours strewn hastily on the brown shag
Her shoes hair braid and a map to the well of souls brimming there

STARK HUNTER

ANTI-POEM 33
"HARRY THE HIPSTER"

(Poet's instruction: Go to YouTube and watch a video performance of Harry the Hipster, before reading this anti-poem).

He is the hippest of the dancing jazz jive
The downest in the cloud of cool razzmatazz
Mister handsome mellow licks swings live
He's the gone-to-town brother clipster
Hey Mister he don't want your jiving sister
He's the handsome handsie Harry the Hipster
Where ya been man I seen your cool striding sister
Where ya been keeping that honey clipster
Hey Mister he's Harry the Hipster playing jazz

Harry the Hipster you'll see him hanging around
Bebop baby wears the inster man, he's in town
Dancing like a crazy cat this way to the clipster
Mister handsome mellow licks he's the cool tipster
He hangs around the club mister jiving the beat
Roasting the piano keys with insane hipster heat
Hey mister Harry the Hipster ain't with your sister
He's playing it boogie woogie style with the clipster
My friend here is the magnificent Harry the Hipster
Striding his dark piano is the handsome jazz lipster
Where ya been man, I seen your jiving blond chickster
Throwing kisses in the direction of a postwar mister

COVID GARDENS

He's the handsome Harry the Hipster playing jiving jazz
He's the downest in the clouds of honky tonk razzmatazz

STARK HUNTER

ANTI-POEM 34
"LINDA KEENE – THE UNLUCKY WOMAN"

(Poet's instruction: Softly play "Unlucky Woman"
by Linda Keene while reading this anti-poem)

I
Stop
Don't go in there
Something smells bad
Madam! May we open the windows?
May we avail ourselves of the frankincense?
May we at least pretend there's nothing
Remotely dead at all in there
Nothing human at least

II
Madam, I knew beforehand of your odd predilections
Your yellow stylings with nascent bananas and acorns
Your inclinations to play phonograph records all night
But will there ever be a time when we can jus' sit here
Relax with a few beers and listen to Linda Keene sing?

III
There she is
Strolling on stage in pageboy obsolescence
It's Linda Keene singing Unlucky Woman
A round of applause please ladies and gentlemen
"Louie, ah, whose Linda Keene? Whose that?"

IV
(She be slinging it down and smooth
Like a wet rolling pin, ya know
Like my auntie would! Hot damn! Go girl!
Waiter! Drinks all around here, and
One hot rum for da' lady up there
She with that bosomy, whiskey-smooth voice
Hey Miss Keene how come nobody heard of ya?
Now she's singing Gershwin with a flashlight
Nobody like Linda Keene nobody)

V
"I just know somebody loves you, honey
And that boy is me, I am that somebody
The road from Wichita Falls to Kalamazoo wheezes
A thousand miles of aching heartbeats and drooping eyes
Will there ever be a time when we can jus' sit there
Inside our own little love shack under those spying stars
Listening with ears and loins to the unlucky woman crooning
Frankie and Johnnie with that crazy jazz band behind her
"My gawd she can sing how come no one heard of her?"
"I loves ya Linda. Loves ya like my own departed mother"
God bless the dead!
"Que eles possam descansar em paz amém" (1)

VI
Will there ever be a time when we can jus' sit here
Have a few beers, relax and do absolutely nothing?
Maybe if you're up to it honey, maybe if there is even
The slightest possibility of our dancing to Linda Keene

STARK HUNTER

You say you never heard of her?
Honey, please sit. Here on my Victrola is Unlucky Woman
Jus' relax, listen and visualize us in a vast field
Visualize the two of us beneath a cedar tree eating
Ripe apples atop a conniving blanket of wild crazy love
Shooting snake eyes twice on a Friday night in the dark

VII
Stop
Don't go in there
Something smells bad
Real bad
Madam, may we open the windows?
May we keep the door ajar for a possible gladiola breeze?
May we at least pretend all is normal and right?
"They don't want us to see it"
"Eles não querem que vejamos" (2)

Poet's notes. Translations for the Portuguese used in this anti-poem:

1) "May they Rest In Peace, amen"
2) "They don't want us to see it"

Linda was the "ide fixe" for this work. Especially her soundie film, "Frankie and Johnnie" from 1942.
Happy to have remembered Linda Keene, great but forgotten singer - 1911-1981.

SH 9/4/20

COVID GARDENS

ANTI-POEM 35
"END OF THE WORLD"

(Poet's instruction: For two minutes visualize riding in a '69 Chevy Caprice in 1969. The Iron Butterfly is playing on the radio. Your sweetheart is sitting close to you as you cruise down the Boulevard).

1
I slow the chevy
then stop.
In A Gadda Da Vida on KHJ
I turn around
and look back.
There, behind the bedroom window,
behind a lacy white curtain,
I see a figure,
a face,
a waving hand,
an old ghost
from a crinkled black and white,
arisen to meet me again,
kiss me again in this darkness,
returning to haunt
my matchboxes and combs,
the pretty Mexican girl
with the black medusa tresses;
She that licked my lips
when pressed against hers;

STARK HUNTER

That is no ghost, or is it?
Let me squint these sated eyes
and double check.
I see the slicker girl of 17 years
dressed in '69 day-glow
dancing to the drum solo again

2
Red girly fingernails
tapping the chevy seat,
always adjusting, turning
dark brown pantyhose,
and the radio,
always planning and conniving
a quick insecure glance
at a perfumed compact.
She opens her purse widely
retrieving the white slicker tube;
Then come the rituals
of lips and tongues and
sweetened spit ensuing there,
'Hey Jude' finding an angular perch
behind them.

3
"Is the door locked?"
Waves of Groucho
on a Magnavox console
emanating towards us
from the next room over

you and me are naked
beneath the whites
ridden in adolescent stains
squirming under the cracks
of raw unfiltered listening
to Pink Floyd smearing alive
the preposterous universe
using Moog synthesizer knives
as Janis from west Texas
sprawls on a ironing board
firmly positioned and plied
She rides the fast horse
two slippery hours ablaze
"Honey, could you turn the dial?"

4
Bill Balance slings eggs and
the Feminine Forum at 3,
riding the waxy airways
with staticky plumes
This dead disc-jockey is
breathing heavily again
into a ghostly microphone.
"Hey Alice, are you a married girl?
Do you have a nice body?
Do you have charging rhino haunches?"

5
"Come inside now.
Hide under these columns,

STARK HUNTER

These stones of plastic marble,
As the world finally ends,
Finally trembles in the sinking sand.
Who knew? Right?
Joke's on us, but honestly,
We all knew it was coming,
Hopefully later, but coming.
Who knew it would happen
Like this?"

I slow the chevy
Then stop.

COVID GARDENS

ANTI-POEM 36
"YOU WANT THAT BURGER?"

(Poet's Instruction: Play "Whiter Shade
Of Pale" by Procol Harum)

Hey, man.
You want that burger?
I'll take them fries too.
Can I have the keys to your jag?
Just kidding, man.
This here chair is mucho uncomfortable.
So, man, you got a couch?
Turn up the Neil Young!
Turn down the Led Zeppelin!
No! I did not have sex with her!
You got me all wrong, man!
Yeah, I took her to Super Burger.
Yeah, I bought her a bag of french fries.
But we didn't do nothing, man.
We just sat talking for a couple hours,
You know, in that sticky booth by the john.
And we talked on and on about, you know, stuff.
Can you dig it, man?
We rapped about God and love and french fries.
And we talked about Procol Harum music!
I kid you not. A Whiter Shade of Pale, man!
Salty Dog, man!
Have you ever heard better sounds, dude?

We did not kiss even once last night.
Look at me, dude!
Do I look like a heel to you?
Dude, I know she's your chick.
I know she's mucho in love with you.
What are these red marks on my neck?
Dude!
Why are you questioning me, man?
Don't go gonzo on me!
These are what you call zits!
Duh, dude!
Red itchy acne.
My mom sent me to a dermatologist for years.
No, man!
I did not lay even one determined finger
Upon your chick's hot sexy body.
Not even one sliver of a glance
From these lonely eyes of mine,
Upon her bitchen-ass tan legs,
Or her puckered pink tulip-lips,
Which I am sure, dude,
Taste like sweet perfume wine.
Meantime I am mucho innocent!
You know I'd never backstab ya!
Hey, man.
You want that burger?

COVID GARDENS

ANTI-POEM 37
"THE SKIES OUTSIDE OOZE"

(Poet's instruction. この指示に従わないでください:
Softly play "Rollin Rock" by the Tielman Brothers,
1960, while reading this anti-poem)

the skies outside ooze smoky choking headaches
once in a while I can hear the big steel monsters
rumble overhead spewing growls and whispers
they ignore the bleeding enchiladas next door
so they turn to the sky-blue tacos at aunt molly's
at daybreak these days they tiptoe to the breakers
with probing noses seeking sour-cream justice pies
given discreetly to the hot-meat sauces bubbling up
stirring forever the gooey sugar islands of false love
of soft repartee with whiskers protruding like knives
all you guys can come to my cool taco island here
spend your needs and your dreams here upon my toe
the skies outside ooze of burned soup on the tappan
now the tiny fruit gnats hover and spin like maniacs
above this fixed board game of intense micro-dancing
the tielmans rocking and rollin to the sinister cymbals
balancing bass chords on electric-banana heartbeats
flying star-bound from here to there not feeling a thing
the skies outside ooze malignant fog drippings on eyelids
more rain-filled consternations turning the yes channel
all you guys can come to my very cool taco pad here
a two bedroom two bath abode of pineapple philosophers

STARK HUNTER

we can pick the dead numbers if you like but I am allergic
we can pray to our pissed-off god for polite annihilations
but now the vultures are here for the backdoor scraps

Post-poem note: (I hope you followed the poet's instruction to not follow his instruction
This piece spurted out of me like a newborn eraserhead. It was inspired by the suffocating California fires this summer, and the overwhelming air pollution).

COVID GARDENS

ANTI-POEM 38
"WOODSTOCK BOOGIE"

(Poet's instruction: Kindly play "Woodstock Boogie"
by Canned Heat at Woodstock, 1969,
while reading this anti-poem)

1z
i feel the rain coming through the red oaks
a sizzling drizzle of electric mind explosions
jumping into the cool air on magic pogo sticks
thumping to the Woodstock Boogie eternal
up there on stage under bright atomic spots

2y
Canned Heat is digging the scene in Bethel
another smoldering joint passes by the brethren
as a stoner copter of peace-bullets trespasses
with mojo soldiers dressed in strange love beads
finding zig-zag nests of long-haired blues children
seizing the zeitgeist with silver alligator clips

3x
the Bear dreaming of the old gigs at the Fillmore
blasting loud blues sonics into the stratosphere
Blind Owl finishing his solo now as the rain falls
still waiting behind stage are my ghost friends
Janis and Jimi toasting champaign to the future
Joe and Richie screaming gonads to be paid now

4w
another army copter finding the rhythm of the toke
immaculate ceremonies under a blue-vested sarong
acid freaks wander the grounds in search of lost friends
Harvey Mandel now throttles up the wah-wah night
cranking a Fender strato-monster in the hard deluge

5v
television star sniffers taste the boiling bouillabaisse
laughing snidely with desiccated martinis dangling
history was made upon these musical pancakes of grass
we all saw it and heard it as the rock gods trembled
heard their fervent anthems of love and peace forever
coming like a cool rain through the red oaks

COVID GARDENS

ANTI-POEM 39
"MISTINGUETT"

(Boldly play "Ca! C'est Paris" by Mistinguett
while reading this anti-poem)

"Je suis la reine de la nuit parisienne"
Jeanne my dear
it is good to see your ostrich plumes
As we sway lazily again
through this arresting coffee garden
These chatty spectacular streets
of breathless garlands and wreathes
The pulsing numberless night lights
with nylon saxophones and satin cymbals
These gesturing nasal steps ascending
to the stone gardens growing there
Sipping golden pilsners by the Seine
Escaping into the violin rooms
redolent of rose lavender and silk as
Silver-plated unicorns fly high
suspended by tied Norman knuckles
Above the ear-buzzing Boulevard de Clichy –
Ahh smell these enticing aromas
dear sweet Jeanne as you dance
As you flirt with white hungry teeth and
dapper copper mustaches
Try the megaphone dearest
not that you need it

STARK HUNTER

May I sleep there
may I be the one tonight my darling
There in your sweet rosy bed
Please dismiss the other boys
hence to the casino floor
Where all the lame birds perch
please my dearest Mistinguett
Show them only your swollen ankles
your bloody toes as you slowly undress
For tonight's dance with the devil
touch them only with your champagne eyes
As you sing to me now
swaying in feathers
"Fais-moi l'amour maintenant enlève mes plumes"

COVID GARDENS

ANTI-POEM 40
"RITA MONTERO"

(Poet's instruction: Kindly play "Ay, Mama Inez"
by Rita Montero while reading this anti-poem)

a red trolley finds Ebbets Field behind a pigtown ditch
significant hotdogs and burnt singles melt into the pitch
Jackie Robinson squares off with an ash tree riding the sky
the flag of our fathers dancing in center field poised to fly

"honey, I hope you like these seats here in the bleachers
you can see Bedford on the phone looking for preachers
an endless parade of white-walled tires scurrying on by
can you smell the Nathan's dogs downstairs on hot rye
let us hurry hence dear, before this inning comes to an end
and our Jackie Robinson comes barreling home to score again"

"Una mujer negra se asoma en el teatro de Buenos Aires"
Argentine goddess with roots in the dark seeping prairies
musically squeezes the brass ring as the black cloud dries
"Rita Montero, you are as lovely as your sweet empanada pies
your wonderful sidewalks through gardens of lapacho trumpets
please come sit with me here, to talk and to eat these crumpets
to speak of your forever glissandos and sad asado whispers
your electric shadows finding humble graces at vespers
retrieving lost spaces from opera teachers and stupid men
to step forward again with singing eyes and a ballpoint pen
Rompiste la puerta blanca maloliente!"

STARK HUNTER

please Rita meet me in Córdoba next Wednesday"

she sits in her bleacher seat with a Nathan's dog on hot rye
"honey, I hope we can see Jackie Robinson hit a deep fly
high up into the airy Brooklyn blue arching yet over Bedford
the democrats in section seven will applaud the proud leopard
Rita Montero, I can see her in the grandstand behind Shotton
she is giving absolution for all the skin sins now long forgotten
let us hurry hence dear, before this inning comes to an end
and our Jackie Robinson comes barreling home to score again"

COVID GARDENS

ANTI-POEM 41
"OUR WINTER LOVE"

(Poet's instruction: Softly play "Our Winter Love" by
Bill Pursell 1963, while reading this anti-poem)

Don't tell me your name
Your identity is not important to me
Your birthdate is non-consequential
But I like your eyes
And the way your brows stretch out
Like tiny rivers of curious fascinations
I sense a shy wind in your soul
As I peer straight into the centers
The miraculous throbbing nexus
Of your pointed chimera eyes
Your rigid filaments drawing me in
Absorbed by an insatiable brace of stones
Don't reveal to me your next thought
Or why your fleeting gestures implode
Into a suborbital release of seismic sighs
I know you are not afraid to grip time
Not afraid to ascend the northern climes
Reach the splendid summits with muted voice
Don't tell me your name
Your identity is not important to me
Your ideas and opinions are non-consequential
But I like your eyes
I feel a sensational winter's love finding us

STARK HUNTER

Ensconced as we are here in this intense ride
Our fingers making wild love in the gloaming
Our stand-up dances behind creaky ashwood
Find a frosted audience of jealous violins
Don't tell me your name
Your soul means nothing to me
Your likes and dislikes are non-consequential
But I like your eyes

COVID GARDENS

ANTI-POEM 42
"FREE FORM GUITAR"

(Poet's Instruction: Play at low volume "Free Form Guitar"
by Terry Kath, 1969, while reading this anti-poem.
Questo è un pezzo oscuro, nessuna scusa;
non ha lo scopo di edificare o elevare l'anima di nessuno)

1
They was the cool guys driving fast
The cool ho-dad cruiser dudes
Swallowing speed-nirvana pills
Rolling fat ones with sullen panache
Sucking on chocolate endorphins and
Drinking isolation martinis with everyone
Now acknowledging the tan chicks kneeling
Pensively adjacent the holy tiled fountains
Seeking to forgive sins with a vengeance
Praying and beseeching in plaid virginal skirts
Seeing ghost epiphanies at midnight mass
Hearing old men singing Latin ditties a cappella
Their placid saintly eyes fluttering as moths do
Winging naively to the pink-clawed capture places
They was the cool dudes driving fast
Cruising hard and slick on the bleak highway
Chicago blasting out Kath's Free Form Guitar
From driveling makeshift speakers spewing
Foaming bricks of electric insanities and fear

STARK HUNTER

2
I have walked through graveyards in the afternoons
Said 'good day' to many friends and enemies alike
All have passed on now to the nearby adjacent rooms
The next round sphere under which we will all reunite
There are no survivors here mama I don't like this place
The living people here are mean mama it's a sick rat race
Nothing has value in this world of deception and mistrust
Everything you once believed in turns to disillusioned dust
Mama I can't stand the stink of this old shoddy motel
Everyone here is in a mad dash controlled by an evil spell
I have strolled through graveyards in the lugubrious night
Said 'good day' to all my dead friends smoking at twilight
All have passed on now to the nearby adjacent rooms
I see them walking to me now dressed in pale costumes

3
static monsters squirming out en masse
exiting from your worst nightmare
erupting like atomic cadaver armies
with foot long belly worms
spiraling into the humbucker fret-holes
a million doors locked now
as Terry Kath sends his regrets
to all the dead hippies in the waxworks
still listening to Hendrix
still mind-tripping from
avalanching mind contusions
the old jams still lacerating the solar plexus
yes music perfect for cocktails and dry tears

COVID GARDENS

are you coming to bed finally
the world has ended deliriously and so
i want your body now all of it
we need to go insane now under these fake skies
these counterfeit hard-ons using yeast pills
time to go inside this fog-induced brain snap
where a dead Groucho again smokes
his impotent limping cigars
broadcasting on a dead television set
beside the steaming static jungles of
bedroom antics after midnight's sauna
johnny is again behind his plywood desk
and you and me are under these white waves
cajoling the sea urchins to swim as they wallow
there terry kath you are the purveyor the master
of this screaming electrocution this nation-wide
hookup this sad soiree with hungry monsters
rampaging filching the bare bones from the fridge
finding naked fish sprawled out in burlap haunches
ready for the butcher and the hardware man
hey terry stop
this is insane I cannot take this
hey, i have opinions

Post poem note: apologies for rhyming the second stanza. The process of rhyming words is an affliction indeed. 4 days in the making. Glad it's done 10/7/20

STARK HUNTER

ANTI-POEM 43
"AUTUMN POSTCARDS"

(Poet's Instruction: Take two Vitamin C supplements with Zinc, plus a Vitamin D and Vitamin K2 supplement as indicated, before reading this anti-poem)

1
Avocado shadows extending over 1931 cement
Mid-October afternoon and football allegiances
Find their knotted shoelaces tied to the television
Quarterback Bill Munson's season is carried out
Strapped on a stretcher into the Coliseum tunnel
These 1965 Rams are losers as I burn the popcorn
The boy's mother is down the hallway in her room
Eating a hamburger with tomato on a white bun
She's in a hurry to finish her dinner before supper
Little Luke Patty is ringing the doorbell repeatedly
He believes no one is home as I ignore his knocking
But the Rams game is showing on CBS channel 2
And staunch Roman Gabriel has taken up the helm

2
I can see him up the street sitting in a lawn chair
Staring straight ahead knowing it is almost over
Mister Nicholson's cancer is up there too reclining
Watching the cars of October swish by the bend
Creating wind eddies which entertain the frail flowers
As kleenex butterflies soar and dip with the silences

COVID GARDENS

Flying out of rushing Fords and pale Chryslers asunder
Sending practiced condolences before the deathbed
Saying a silent studied farewell to the staring neighbors
What memory monsters did he confront those last days
To what hole or rampart could he seek a final reprieve
Can you see the skinny Mister Nicholson up the street
There on his front lawn dancing his wedding waltz again

3
The boy's mother is down the hallway in her room
Groaning in gall bladder agony atop her blue 1964 bed
Goldwater is speaking on a very segregated television set
As Huntley and Brinkley serve up another smorgasbord
Of Lyndon Baines quips addressing the teamsters' manholes
Brought to us by the makers of the Industrial military complex
And Anacin for fast pain relief and numbed-out tomorrows
Little Luke Patty is ringing the doorbell repeatedly again
He believes no one is home as I ignore his knocking
The boy's mother slowly strolls the hospital promenade
Arm in arm with Doctor Evers after the segregated surgery
They both seem to think it is the end of the world
I follow behind wearing catholic shoes and scapulars

4
There were orange pastel drippings that October eve
Streaking the horizon's backhand with pumpkin grease
The boy and his freckled neighbor toted two stout bags
No finer plunder had Captain Kidd himself parlayed as
Sweetly as these jewels and chewy gemstones given freely
By nurturing pirates and loving monsters wearing aprons

STARK HUNTER

Now the ghost of Big Bad John seeps wily through the elms
As a host of zombie children zig-zag upon the lighted doors
The boy's freckled neighbor fills with robust effort two bags
Overflowing with the sweet creamy wonders of this world
Every kind of candy bar and stout-worthy treat imaginable
Then upon the 9 o'clock hour when most pirates are asleep
Teenage frankensteins in a hot rod filched the freckled night

5
Little Luke Patty on this smog-laced afternoon rings the doorbell
He rings its repeatedly over and over as with all toxic rain drops
Pummeling incessantly the idea that all such ringings are invited
Not wishing to further ignore this blond six year old boy asunder
I opened said door that October day to find a cosmic smile gaping
Whereupon the boy took Little Luke Patty to climb the garage ladder
Out back amongst the Valencias and the aluminum trash cans
Next door the pulsating sounds of a radio revealed Do Wah Diddy
Flying through the avocado leaves like gawking spirits teasing
Then as Little Luke Patty ascends the splintery ladder to the clouds
A cosmic misstep brings the child asunder falling as a dove descends
Bringing an erupting painful cry as his head hits the sidewalk cement
Now the spirit angels hover like thirsty dragonflies in a summer rain

6
The boy's mother is down the hallway in her room
Eating a grilled cheese sandwich on white Weber's bread
Sonny and Cher are singing on a long-haired black and white
Deciding maybe it is to time for history to turn the page
Driving up the street in a '58 Fairlane is Mister Nicholson
Bespectacled frail and wearing a white shirt and black tie

COVID GARDENS

Now we see him hugging his daughter as he exits the Ford
An avenue of clocks and doorbells continues to pulsate on
Boeing behemoths groan across the skies like winged hotels
Bringing in country fried pilgrims with transistor radio eyes
The boy's mother is down the hallway in her room
Gazing out her sad window at the dying Mister Nicholson
As kleenex butterflies soar and dip with the silences

STARK HUNTER

ANTI-POEM 44
"MONA LISA"

("Poet's Instruction: Softly play "Mona Lisa" by Nat King Cole from 1950 while reading this anti-poem)

No Lisa. I am not afraid.
Where on my sleeve do I shine yellow?

You are the choicest of life's pastries.
The universe has a hard-on for you,
As I do now here at the end of the world.
But as you sit there as my eternal lover,
Your stringent expectations surpassing,
My abilities to even unfold my capacities,
I wonder if this is even appropriate now
As millions drown in the hateful gurgling.

Maybe we can sit here instead and pray.
Maybe we should close our eyes and listen.

The survivors now are creating their mad gods,
With mindless verve and pleasing contours;
These robot monster hybrids singing arias,
Making false speeches to the groveling captives.

Mona Lisa! Mona Lisa! Go home to your mother.
She fell in the bathtub butt-first and is stuck.
We sent for the pill salesman to get her out but

COVID GARDENS

Well, there you have it.

No, Lisa. I am not afraid.
I am looking into the green cemetery now
and I can see God.
He is digging up the dead with a bloody pickaxe.

STARK HUNTER

ANTI-POEM 45
"SILENT MERCIES"

(Poet's Instruction: Softly play in the background
Mario Lanza singing "Your Tiny Hand Is Frozen" from
Puccini's La Boheme, while reading this anti-poem)

A
Look over there.
See the stunned grandmother knitting,
Not speaking a word neither, nor listening,
Pretending she's okay when she isn't.
Notice the moribund listing grandfather,
Deep in his leather chair, stroked-stricken, pissing,
In deep shock over the heap of blood and brains,
Sitting cold and raw on the floor of his bedroom.
His sad grandson Jack Judy has visited today at noon,
Has repeatedly knocked on the rusty screen door,
On this faraway day crying tears in a crazed 1971,
Seeking for his sad frozen hand a hot groveling gun.

B
Look over there.
Cruising down Carmenita in a fast Volkswagen,
Driving in rushed shock behind trudging Fords,
The bearded hippie kid, bare-footed and tanned,
Arrives without shirt to a hushed crowd of busy cops,
Huddling and questioning the knitting grandmother;
A stale Big Mac sits dry and dead on a pink TV tray.

COVID GARDENS

"Mam, can you tell us what happened here today?"
"Well, he said he was tired and went into that room.
That's when he took the pistol and shot hisself."
Then the hippie kid barefooted and meddling there,
Felt the breaking of his naked toe under a busy boot.
"Do you need to be here? It's time to go elsewhere."

C
Look over there.
See the hippie kid's dead cousin on the floor.
The stoic grandmother is channeling the Sylvania,
La Boheme from the Metropolitan Opera House,
As a wailing ambulance streaks down Carmenita.
"He's in there I think he's dead he shot hisself!"
"Che gelida manina, se la lasci riscaldar.
Cercar che giova? Al buio non si trova."
As with the loading of a burlap consecration,
The dead cousin receives a newer absolution.
Notice the moribund listing grandfather there,
Ensconced in his last high chair dripping urine,
"Who gunna clean 'dat mess, woman? I can't!"

D
Look over there.
See the hippie kid's father chauffeuring the wife,
Cruising down Carmenita in a fast Chevy caprice,
Driving in disbelieving shock behind slow Oldsmobiles,
Arrives with gloves, bucket, mop and silent mercies.
Notice the dying listing grandfather staring at the floor,
Ensconced there in his big moribund chair not listening.

STARK HUNTER

See the traumatized grandmother knitting by the door,
The stale Big Mac still sitting dead on the pink TV tray.
"Mama, please tell me what happened here today."
"Well, he said he was tired and went into the room.
That's when he took the pistol and shot hisself."
See the hippie kid's father silently wiping up the gore.

Post-anti-poem notes: This piece is a memory excursion with a tad bit of rhyming.
My apologies for this contrivance.
This anti-poem is true.
Translation of the Italian: (by Tom Thomson)
"What a frozen little hand,
let me warm it up.
what use is looking?
In the dark we won't find it"
(from La Boheme by Giacomo Puccini)

COVID GARDENS

ANTI-POEM 46
"SCREAMING REQUIEMS"

(Poet's Instruction: Due to coronavirus concerns, all readers are strongly encouraged to not read this anti-poem. Unless you keep six feet distant)

Z
Intricate undulations caress the lascivious moanings.
Cascading brain waves ascend the soft pinnacles.
Descending purple silhouettes spin inert pirouettes.
Plunging earthward now through eye-trees uprooted.
Huge sneeze tsunamis blow athwart the earth's nose.

Y
City dancers levitating and aspirating icy body parts.
Ululating sex machines reach back for lace aspirins,
Downing doses of afternoon shenanigans aquivering.
Penis and Vagina exchanging fond correspondences.
Their wedding day trundling with sauces and cheeses.

X
She-meat dust-sitters pander to three digging dogs.
She-dudes wearing button-shades slyly commiserate.
Leviathan girls rush out from within the oiled barracks,
Exchanging nil phone numbers under a seducing bridge.
Newspaper mongrels sniffing the boilers and the beefcake.

STARK HUNTER

W

Squeezed pomegranates lie recumbent on salty ledges.
Screaming requiems consecrate the body and the blood.
They pillage and procreate with indignant eviscerations.
Mother madness machines encroaching the battlements.
Bloody rainbow-fixations sautéing the night movements.

V

Gertrude Stein reads scribbled postcards in the Père Lachaise.
Earthworm diagnostics supplant the rum-filled remediations.
This boarded-up bistro by the Seine is now serving the dead.
Embalmed waitresses stand like steel ostriches taking orders,
Their rolling black eyes revealing the fiery flesh pits of Pau.

Je fermerais la fenêtre, mais il n'y a pas de fenêtre.
11/3/20

Il est temps pour une pause toilettes maintenant.

COVID GARDENS

ANTI-POEM 47
"SUGAR PLUMS"

(Poet's instruction: Play at low volume, Patsy Cline, singing "I Fall To Pieces" from 1961, while reading this anti-poem.)

Okay, okay.
I hear ya.
Just wake me up from your crazy nightmare,
Whenever.

There ain't no happy endings, sugar plums.
All them dudes, five of 'em, got left in the dust.
Lucas McCain was in town with that rifle of his.

Yeah, these sure are strange times in the world.
I seen Perry Mason canvassing the neighborhood,
He was with that dame Della Street again last night,
They was under that mulberry tree there, kissing.

Okay, okay.
I hear ya.
I won't smoke no more in the house!
Hey, who do ya' think pays the rent on this pad?
Well, it ain't the Man from Planet X.
Seventy-five bucks a month, sugar plums!
Hey, where's ma' hamburger and french fries?
Ya' mean you ain't gone yet?

STARK HUNTER

Okay, okay,
I hear ya.
I'll take my feet off the table.
I seen Pete's wife, Gladys.
Imagine that happening in 1961?
She ain't dead in the basement after all!

Is that Patsy Cline on the radio now?
Wow, I Fall To Pieces is so sad, sugar plums.
She sings like my dead mother out back there.
Hey, are you going to Super Burger or not?
Pick up an order of them onion rings while you're there.

No I'm not seeing no one else, sugar plums.
How can you ask that?
I'm an innocent man, honey!
No, that is not a hickey on my neck.
How many times do I have to tell you that?
Sugar plums, you are the only one!
You are my princess of the stick shift!
Jus' wake me up from your trip to
The Twilight Zone,
Whenever.

COVID GARDENS

ANTI-POEM 48
"MOTHER DEAREST"

(Poet's Instruction: Softly play in the background,
"Mother Dearest, Mother Fairest" by the Singing Nuns, 2012)

Mother dearest, I am ashamed to say,
We are the imminently mesmerized,
The hypnotized, and the bamboozled.
Plead with us in your drywall paradise,
Make sure we, your children, do our lessons.
Indeed, for we are the haplessly hoodwinked,
The fervently swindled and the beguiled.
We are the confused ones and the rooked.
Mother dearest, forever hanging your wash,
Dry our gullible tears now with a clean hanky,
For we are the righteously hornswoggled,
The stunned and the piously deluded;
Talk to us here in your smooth mohair cave,
The seriously swindled and the speeved.
Deliver us with your watchful attentions.
Your hawk-eyed apprehensions, of us and them,
The deliriously duped and the defrauded.
Indeed, we are your dull fools with tin brains,
The irrepressibly snookered; the dude-busted.
Mother dearest, turning in your high heaven,
Feed us now your dangling truth-berries,
Your drooping flesh glaciers of owl realities;.
For we have been immaculately flimflammed,

STARK HUNTER

Rapturously and obediently imposed upon.
Mother dearest, please deliver us from here,
For your children are the haplessly bamboozled,
The forever hornswoggled, with dull tin brains.

COVID GARDENS

ANTI-POEM 49
"SO RARE"

(Poet's instruction: Please play in the background, "So Rare"
by Jimmy Dorsey, 1957, while reading this anti-poem)

In 1957
I would lie alone on the green suburban lawn
Parceled out with rebar in front of our small house,
And listen intently to the silver constellations flying by
I'd listen to the blaring propellers spinning distantly
Carving out sound monsters against the postwar sky
And looking south through an orange curtain of air
I could hear the voices of the fading past intoning
Stretching out the stubborn day to its last heartbeat
One final metallic sunset blast stretching LA to heaven
Spreading it out for all the living loud places to hear
"So rare. You have the warmth of a Schubert air,
Charming and debonair."

But listen
Can you hear jimmy Dorsey playing So Rare
Playing like a wailing jazz-siren from the highest granite peak
Jimmy embracing that sweet sax as one would a ripe lover
Outside on the lit highways of America I can hear him playing
Intrepid brass spires of hopeful prayer and fearful resignation
Lifting everyone up still, saying this new life is good and true
"You are perfection you're my idea,
Of angels singing the Ave Maria."

STARK HUNTER

But now
Jimmy Dorsey is serenading the dead at Glen Island
All the platter masters before him sending their sad solo riffs
Their heartbreaking tessellations of life, love and longing
Play on sir, play on
Now in your bow-tied paradise of unending exaltations
"Those are the words for you."

(Post anti-poem note: Lyrics included in this work are by Jack Sharpe, Published 1937).

COVID GARDENS

ANTI-POEM 50
"LAST NIGHT"

(Poet's Instruction: Play at low volume, "Last Night" by
the Mar-Keys, 1961, while reading this anti-poem)

Coma girls arrive
With taco-dressed bunion squeezers
Looking to decide about last night
And the recessed peppermint stink
Smothering the chestnut streets
With playtex man-eaters attired in
Green, lavender and cost-effective mauve
With rich pliers unscrewing the salvation bibles
Absorbing like old wood the truth bar
Sweaty-chinned nuns with lace guns
Spray a new kind of blood paint,
Manufactured in Tuskegee
With crawling smokestack seductions
Fingering the grapefruit entanglements
Amidst a chorus of deft acclamations
They say we are in love with charlatans
These big-chested somethings
With nothing brains
The coma girls know nothing
They see nothing
I see my dead mother watering the flowers.
As the world sleeps at last
For it is high time

STARK HUNTER

To turn the screw again
Time to suck in
The stinking blood money
The thieving ash pit and
You turning it
For the right to cancel my soul
As it freely departs
These musty cramped spaces,
These sweet-guitar princess places, we
Standing naked amidst the static and the
Reverb nothing places
This world is nothing as I am nothing
In this taco hole-in-the-wall
In sunny Reseda
Where my senorita girl lives upstairs there
She's strutting down old avenues now
With the Aunt Jemima choirs
Screaming their death anthems
See as they roll up the sidewalks
Like parchment membranes
Crying out with justice candles
For now it is not enough
Like last night with you and me
A heavy salad before the soup
As the world is ending playfully now
Here, in my childhood backyard
I see ghosts and shadows of my past
I see my dead mother watering the flowers.

COVID GARDENS

ANTI-POEM 51
"MIASMA CLOUDS"

(Poet's Instruction: Readers, before reading this anti-poem, please close your eyes for one minute and imagine walking alone in an old cemetery. Imagine hearing voices from the shadows.

Leser, bevor Sie dieses anti-poem lesen, schließen Sie bitte eine Minute lang die Augen und stellen Sie sich vor, Sie gehen alleine auf einem alten Friedhof. Stellen Sie sich vor, Sie hören Stimmen aus den Schatten).

Miasma clouds hovering like frosted cotton fields.
The meat people sip white whales at a bleeding bar,
Talking, deciding what to do at the end of the world.
Dead auntie has radiation syrup in her musty cupboard,
And dead grandmother's false teeth in a glittering jar.
Shall we mosey beyond these old wheezing terraces,
These skinless inner hallways of the still blue ménage,
And seek the gaping escape window to the garden isle?
There we will find the eternal ghost people making love,
Under pale moist sheets made of regrets and orgasms.
Now creeping up on Hoggett Lane and Gunster Road,
I see dead flowers strewing themselves to the watchers.
Alive again in the old houses downstream in the rushes;
They are astonished in their slow deathless maundering.

STARK HUNTER

ANTI-POEM 52
"THE POEM THAT DOES NOT EXIST"

(Poet's Instruction: anti-poem 52 does not exist. At least it does not exist inside this volume. Kindly examine the picture on this last page of Covid Gardens.

After 10 minutes, please write your own anti-poem. Kindly process the poem on a computer, and publish it on-line).

Photo by Hunter

COVID GARDENS

THE LAST PAGE
"C'EST LA FIN DE TOUT CELA. S'IL TE PLAIT FERME LA FENÊTRE."

'Hey baby! This jam is done! Yeah! So hey! Where's the party? What's happening later?
Where's the chicks? Yah baby, we can go to Jimmy's pad and trip on some dime. Jimmy
baby is the man! He's the one! Yah man!"
`` ¡Oye bebé! Este atasco se acabó. ¡Si! ¡Oye! ¿Donde es la fiesta? ¿Qué está pasando
después, o quizás ahora mismo? ¿Dónde están las chicas? Sí, cariño, podemos ir al
piso de Jimmy y tropezar con algo de dinero. ¡Jimmy baby es el hombre! ¡Él es el único!
¡Si hombre!"
"It is not everyday that the world arranges itself into a poem."

—Wallace Stevens

Photo by Hunter

ABOUT THE AUTHOR

Born in Whittier, California in 1952, Stark Hunter was a high school English teacher for 34 years before retiring from the classroom in 2017. He has written and published 11 books, which are available on Amazon.com and Barnes & Noble.com: In A Gadda Da Vida, a novel, published in 2002, Carnivorous Avenues, a poetry volume published in 2004, Flies, a short novel published in 2005, Private Diaries, a satire published in 2006, Voices From Clark Cemetery, a poetry volume published in 2013, Cocktails For the Soul, a poetry anthology published in 2013, Voices From Mt. Olive Cemetery, a poetry volume published in 2018, Digested by the Dust, another poetry anthology, published in 2018, Scenes From the Cerebellum, published in 2019, Monster Trees, published in 2020, and White Sidewalks in 2021. Mr. Hunter's poetry has been included in the following Poetry Anthologies: Stars In Our Hearts, Visions, published 2012 (World Poetry Movement); In My Lifetime, Chronicles, published 2013 (Eber and Wein Publishing); PS: It's Poetry,

COVID GARDENS

An Anthology Of Eclectic Contemporary Poems Written By Poets From Around the Globe, published 2020 (PoetrySoup.Com). Three of the author's poems were read on Diverse TV with host, Alexandro Botelho, for his program, "Live Writings On The Wall" in 2021. Fourteen of Mr. Hunter's poems from Voices From Clark Cemetery were adopted and set to music by Dr. George Mabry, composer and former conductor of the Nashville Symphony Chorus, for his work, Voices, a musical drama which was performed at Austin Peay State University in Clarksville, Tennessee in 2015. Mr. Hunter's poetry works can be perused at poetrysoup.com. and allpoetry.com. Mr. Hunter is married with two daughters, a granddaughter, and resides in Chino Hills, California.

www.ingramcontent.com/pod-product-compliance
Lightning Source LLC
Chambersburg PA
CBHW020940090426
42736CB00010B/1205